GERVASE PHINN

Teaching Poetry
in the Primary Classroom

Crown House Publishing Limited
www.crownhouse.co.uk – www.crownhousepublishing.com

First published by
Crown House Publishing Ltd
Crown Buildings, Bancyfelin, Carmarthen, Wales, SA33 5ND, UK
www.crownhouse.co.uk
and
Crown House Publishing Company LLC
6 Trowbridge Drive, Suite 5, Bethel, CT 06801, USA
www.crownhousepublishing.com

British Library of Cataloguing-in-Publication Data
A catalogue entry for this book is available
from the British Library.

10-digit ISBN 184590130-4
13-digit ISBN 978-184590130-1

LCCN 2008936754

Printed and bound in the UK by
Cam[   ]   , Cambridge

Contents

I think that poetry should surprise by fine excess and not by singularity—it should strike the reader as a reading of his own highest thoughts, and appear almost a remembrance. Its touches of beauty should never be halfway, thereby making the reader breathless instead of content; the rise, the progress, the setting of imagery should like the sun come natural to him—shine over him and set soberly although in magnificence leaving him in the luxury of twilight—but it is easier to think what poetry should be than to write it—and this leads me on to another axiom. That if poetry comes not as naturally as the leaves to a tree it had better not come at all.

John Keats in a Letter to John Taylor, 27 February 1818

Poetry has great educative power, but in many schools it suffers from lack of commitment, misunderstanding, and the wrong kind of orientation. There are few more rewarding experiences in all English teaching than when the teacher and pupil meet in the enjoyment of a poem.

A Language for Life: The Bullock Report

Poetry is a most wonderful art: to read, to listen to, to attempt. It takes the gift of language and pays it the respect of fashioning it into the finest forms while retaining a grip on the human-measure of life. For many, it is dinned into their unwilling heads at school, trailed across their noses in restless adolescence and ever after considered a part of another world. Not the real ordinary world. Yet the real world has been the poet's prime concern. And many of us believe that the real world has been represented more accurately and powerfully by poets than by anyone else.

Melvyn Bragg in *How to Enjoy Poetry* by Vernon Scannell

If I read a book [and] it makes my whole body feel so cold no fire can ever warm me, I know *that* is poetry. If I feel physically as if the top of my head were taken off, I know *that* is poetry.

Emily Dickinson in *How to Read a Poem: And Fall in Love with Poetry* by Edward Hirsch

The fact that I still recall poems with ease and can delight in them as verbal music means that they were bedding the ear with a kind of linguistic hard core that could be built on some day.

Seamus Heaney in *Seamus Heaney: The Crisis of Identity* by Floyd Collins

Chapter 1
Creating the Environment

'I'm very good at poetry you know.'

The speaker, with all the honesty, enthusiasm and confidence of an eight year old, was called Helen. I met her on my visit to an infant school to look at the range of writing undertaken by the children.

'Would you like to see my poems?' she continued.

'I would love to,' I replied.

She smiled. 'I'll fetch my portfolio.'

Helen was right—she was good at poetry. Her folder of poems contained a colourful description of the local canal: *straight and long like the dark green stalk of a tall tulip*; a holiday memory featuring her father *who growled and grunted, sighed and shouted when the car would not start*; rhyming verse about the supermarket where the shelves were full of *packets of sugar and cans of beans, Bananas and apples and tangerines, Carrots and onions, potatoes and greens*, and the thoughts of a Roman soldier, *cold and alone and away from home*. I asked if I could make a copy of her latest poem.

'If you wait a minute,' she said, 'I'll give you a print out.'

Here is her lively descriptive verse:

From the school window
I can see where a mole has been burrowing.
The field is lumpy with little brown hills of soil.
Down below where it's dark and damp,
He digs and digs with big flat paws,
Looking for a juicy worm.

'Do you write poetry?' Helen asked, handing me a copy of her poem.

'Yes I do,' I replied.

'Do you get the rhythms?'

'Yes.'

'And the rhymes?'

'Sometimes.'

'Do you illustrate your poems?'

'No, I'm afraid I don't.'

She smiled. 'I do,' she said, 'I think it makes them look nicer on the page.'

'And why are you so good at writing poetry?' I asked.

She sighed. 'Oh, I don't really know. I like to read them. We have lots of poetry books in our classroom. Our teacher likes poems and she reads a poem to us every day after she's marked the register and we always write a poem when we do our topic.'

With this kind of environment and encouragement it should come as no surprise that Helen is such an accomplished poet. Helen's teacher is an enthusiast and her passion for poetry is infectious. Listed below are some of the things she does to keep herself well-informed and to encourage her pupils to enjoy, appreciate and understand the poetry she presents to them.

1. Provides a wide selection of good, appropriate poetry anthologies in the book corner of the classroom. This collection includes pop-up books, nursery rhymes, modern and traditional anthologies, scripts and poems for reading aloud, verse on tape, poetry posters and cards.

2. Reads a wide selection of poems to the children over the year: poems that make the children laugh, think and feel sad, poems with strong rhythms and gentle lyrics, verse from Africa, Asia, Australia and the US, as well as from the British Isles.

3. Allows some time for the children to browse among the poetry and reading books and for them to read poems quietly, listen to them on tape and read the poems of other children.

4. Collects the children's poems—some hand-written and illustrated, others word-processed—in a class anthology.

5. Encourages the children to keep a special book for writing in their favourite poems.

6. Collects together her own favourite poems in a folder and compiles a list, which she adds to regularly, of poetry suitable for the children.

7. Encourages the children to keep a special folder (the portfolio) of their own poems.

8. Reads a short, entertaining or challenging poem each day. Sometimes she encourages the pupils to talk about the poem but on other occasions nothing is said—the children just enjoy the experience.

9. Integrates poetry into the topic work the children undertake.

10. Uses poems for handwriting practice.

11. Encourages the children to perform their own poems and published verse in the classroom and at assembly.

12. Enters children for poetry competitions.

13. Encourages children to learn poems by heart.

14   Invites writers into school to work with the children and share their experience of the process of writing—where their ideas come from, the research they have to undertake, how they draft and revise, proof-read and submit for publication.

15   Organises Book Weeks during which teachers, parents, writers and advisers visit the school to contribute to the various activities.

16   Mounts colourful and interesting displays of the children's poetry in the classroom and along the corridors.

17   Shows children how real poets draft, redraft, alter, edit and refine their work.

18   Talks to the children about poetic techniques and devices: rhythm, rhyme, imagery, contrast, repetition, figures of speech, as they arise in the poems she reads to them and in the children's own efforts.

19   Uses paintings, line drawings, photographs, drama and music as stimuli for the children's poetic writing.

20   Encourages the children to write in a range of structures: snapshot poems, haiku, alphabet poems, concrete verse, acrostics, limericks, riddles, free and rhyming verse.

21   Keeps up with her reading of poetry by visiting the School Library Service HQ, being a member the Poetry Society, reading the reviews in *The School Librarian* and other journals and keeping in close and regular contact with local bookshops.

Providing this sort of rich and stimulating environment is essential if poetry is to flourish. In addition children need specific guidance and ideas to start them off. It is not enough to merely give children a topic and expect them to write a poem.

Over the years as a teacher, adviser, school inspector and visiting poet, I have worked with primary and infant school teachers and their pupils in an effort to give poetry a higher profile, promote its enjoyment and appreciation, and encourage the children to write a range of verse. The following suggestions are distilled from the work I have undertaken in schools.

Chapter 2

Reading Poetry with Infants

There is no doubt that the combination of rhythm, rhyme and striking illustration brings the reader the closest to a successful and satisfying reading that he or she has ever known. The lines unfold effortlessly once the text has been heard once or twice and the new reader experiences a flow and fluency that may hitherto have been elusive. Then the reader is liberated to enjoy poetry's particular way of saying things.

Judith Graham and Elizabeth Plackett, *Developing Readers*

When they arrive at the infant classroom many children will have had some experience of poetry. They will have heard television jingles and know some of the popular nursery rhymes. At playgroup or in the nursery some will have been introduced to poems with lively rhythms, strong rhymes, choruses and repetition and been encouraged, as they sit together on the carpet, to take part—often adding actions and mimes. The infant teacher will draw on this experience and those children who have learnt rhymes by heart will delight in performing them. Many will know the popular nursery rhymes: 'Humpty Dumpty', 'Jack and Jill', 'Georgie Porgy', 'Simple Simon' and 'Little Bo-Peep' but be unfamiliar with such nursery verse as 'Good King Arthur', 'Jack-a-Nory', 'As I was Going to St Ives' and 'They That Wash on Monday'. The teacher might introduce the children to some of these old and unusual rhymes by encouraging them to join in with the chorus:

THE FARMER AND THE RAVEN

A farmer went trotting,
Upon his grey mare,
Bumpety, Bumpety, Bump!
With his daughter behind him,
So rosy and fair,
Lumpety, Lumpety, Lump!

A raven cried: 'Croak!'
And they all tumbled down,
Bumpety, Bumpety, Bump!
The mare broke her knees,
And the farmer his crown,
Lumpety, Lumpety, Lump!

The mischievous raven,
Flew laughing away,
Bumpety, Bumpety, Bump!
And vowed he would serve them
The same the next day,
Bumpety, Bumpety, Bump!

Once they are familiar with the traditional nursery rhymes the teacher might read some alternatives. Here are a few of mine:

'Mary, Mary, quite contrary,
How does your garden grow?'
'I suggest you read a gardening book,
And then you'll get to know!'

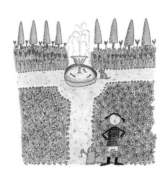

Jack and Jill went up the hill,
Their feet they felt like lead.
Said Jack, 'Oh, let's not bother, Jill,
We'll go to town instead.'

Little Miss Mabel,
Sat at the table,
Eating her curry and rice.
There came down a snake
Which swallowed her plate,
Which really was not very nice.

Little Miranda sat on the veranda
Having a noonday nap.
There buzzed down a bee
Which sat on her knee,
And Miranda said, 'Ooh, fancy that!'

Humpty Dumpty sat on a wall.
Humpty Dumpty had a great fall.
He didn't shout and he didn't scream,
For below him was a trampoline.

(Published in *What I Like! Poems for the Very Young*
by Gervase Phinn, Child's Play International)

The teacher could supplement the nursery rhymes with other popular repetitive verse:

TWENTY-FOUR ROBBERS

Not last night but the night before …
Twenty-four robbers
Came a-knocking at my door,
I asked them what they wanted,
And this is what they said …
H … O … T… hot peppers!!!

FLYING MY KITE

My kite on the ground
Is paper and string,
But up in the sky
It will dance and will sing.
A kite in the sky
Will twirl and will caper,
But back on the ground
Is just string and brown paper.

MARY

One, two, three, four,
Mary's at the cottage door.
She's eating cherries off a plate,
Five, six, seven, eight.

LADYBIRD

Ladybird, ladybird,
Fly away home,
Your house is on fire,
Your children are gone.
Ladybird, ladybird,
Lost and alone,
No family to care for,
No work to be done.

WHISKY FRISKY SQUIRREL

Whisky, frisky, hipperty hop,
Up he goes,
To the tall tree top!

Whirly, twirly, round and round,
Down he scampers
To the ground.

Furly, curly, what a tail,
Tall as a feather
And broad as a sail.

Where's his supper?
In the shell.
Snappy, cracky, out it fell!

Young children love chanting this traditional and highly rhythmic verse:

IN A DARK, DARK WOOD!

In a dark, dark wood
There was a dark, dark house,
And in that dark, dark house
There was a dark, dark room,
And in that dark, dark room
There was a dark, dark cupboard,
And in that dark, dark cupboard

There was a dark, dark shelf,
And on that dark, dark shelf
There was a dark, dark box,
And in that dark, dark box
There is a little furry mouse.

I have given this old tale a new twist in one of my own poems which older infant children have performed with gusto:

IN A DARK, DARK TOWN!

In a dark, dark town,
There was a dark, dark street,
And in that dark, dark street,
There was a dark, dark school,
And in that dark, dark school,
There were these dark, dark gates,
And behind those dark, dark gates,
There was a dark, dark door,
And beyond that dark, dark door,
There was a dark, dark corridor,
And down that dark, dark corridor,
There was a dark, dark classroom,
And in that dark, dark classroom,
There was a dark, dark desk,
And in that dark, dark desk,
There was a dark, dark drawer,
And in that dark, dark drawer,
There was a dark, dark box,
And in that dark, dark box,
There was ...
Colin Cooper's conker which Miss Cawthorne confiscated
Because he was playing with it in class.

(Published in *Don't Tell the Teacher*
by Gervase Phinn, Puffin)

Here is another example of my repetitive verse for children to perform:

THIS IS THE KEY

This is the key of the school.
In that school there is a classroom.
In that classroom there is a desk.
In that desk there is a drawer.
In that drawer there is a box.
In that box are my sweets.
Which Mrs Davis confiscated yesterday.
Sweets in the box,
Box in the drawer,
Drawer in the desk,
Desk in the room,
Room in the school.
This is the key to the school.
Decisions! Decisions!

(Published in *What I Like! Poems for the Very Young*
by Gervase Phinn, Child's Play International)

There is a wide variety of action rhymes available in the collections I recommend later on, where children can join in with the teacher with body movements, expressions, hands and fingers. Favourites are: 'This is the Church and this is the Steeple', 'This Little Piggy Went to Market', 'Incy Wincy Spider', 'The Wheels on the Bus', 'Round and Round the Garden', 'There's a Flippy Floppy Scarecrow', 'The House that Jack Built' and 'Five Little Speckled Frogs'. A board book sure to delight young children and which demands their participation is Annie Kubler's *Head, Shoulders, Knees and Toes*, published in a range of different languages by Mantra Lingua. Children love to hold their heads, shake their shoulders, rub their knees and tickle their toes, singing along with the familiar chorus.

Here is a counting rhyme of my own based on the traditional poem 'Five Little Owls':

FIVE LITTLE OWLS

Five little owls in an old oak tree,
Fluffy and puffy as owls could be,
Blinking and winking with big round eyes
At the big round moon that hangs in the skies.
As I passed by I could hear one say,
'There'll be mouse for supper, there will, today!'
Then all of them hooted, 'Tu-whit, tu-whoo,
Yes, mouse for supper, hoo hoo, hoo hoo!'

In my poem 'Five Fat Conkers' children hold their fingers downward to represent conkers, leaves, berries, acorns and the boy, and then they wiggle them as they blow on them and drop their hands onto their laps!

FIVE FAT CONKERS

Five fat conkers on the chestnut tree,
Were dangling down for all to see.

Whoosh! came the wind, blowing through the town,
And five fat conkers came tumbling down!

Four green leaves on the sycamore tree,
Were dangling down for all to see.

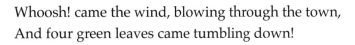

Whoosh! came the wind, blowing through the town,
And four green leaves came tumbling down!

Three red berries on the rowan tree,
Were dangling down for all to see.

Whoosh! came the wind, blowing through the town,
And three red berries came tumbling down!

Two round acorns on the old oak tree,
Were dangling down for all to see.

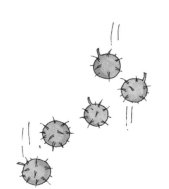

Whoosh! came the wind, blowing through the town,
And two round acorns came tumbling down!

One small boy in the willow tree,
Was dangling down for all to see.

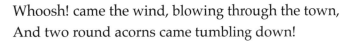

Whoosh! came the wind, blowing through the town,
And one small boy came tumbling down!

(Published in *What I Like! Poems for the Very Young*
by Gervase Phinn, Child's Play International)

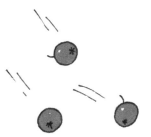

Young children love the challenge of the tongue-twister. 'She Sells Sea Shells' and 'Peter Piper' are particular favourites and children love reciting 'I Saw Esau', 'Night Lights' and 'Whether the Weather':

I SAW ESAU

I saw Esau sawing wood,
And Esau saw I saw him;
Though Esau saw I saw him saw,
Still Esau went on sawing.

NIGHT LIGHTS

There is no need to light a nightlight
On a light night like tonight;
For a nightlight's light's a slight light
When the moonlight's white and bright.

WHETHER THE WEATHER

Whether the weather be fine
Or whether the weather be not,
Whether the weather be cold
Or whether the weather be hot—
We'll weather the weather
Whatever the weather
Whether we like it or not!

Here is a tongue-twister of my own:

DAVID DRAPER

 David Draper dropped a dozen delicious donuts.

A dozen delicious donuts David Draper dropped.

If David Draper dropped a dozen
delicious donuts,

Where's the dozen delicious donuts
David Draper dropped?

Daisy, David Draper's dribbling dog,
devoured them!

That's what!

(Published in *What I Like! Poems for the Very Young*
by Gervase Phinn, Child's Play International)

Infant teachers might introduce young children to some new and inventive poems full of engaging humour, lively language, catchy rhymes and strong regular rhythms. Poems like:

- *The Parrot Tico Tango*, written and illustrated by Anna Witte, Barefoot. In this beautifully illustrated picture book full of lush tropical colours and catchy rhymes, the greedy parrot steals the fruit from his friends until he carries so much he drops the lot.

- *My Granny Went to Market*, written by Stella Blackstone and illustrated by Christopher Corr, Barefoot. An adventurous Granny travels around the world on her magic carpet, shopping everywhere she goes.

- *Hairy Maclary* by Lynley Dodd, Puffin.

- 'The Sock' by Carol Ann Duffy in her collection *The Hat*, Faber & Faber.

- 'It's My Bedroom' by Jenny Sullivan and 'Summer Holidays' by Francesca Kay in *Look Out! Poems for Children*, chosen by Neil Nuttall and Andy Hawkins, and illustrated by Kay Widdowson, Pont.

- 'Shell' and 'Chips' by Ruth Morgan in *Jumping the Waves: Sglod's Favourite Poems* by Ruth Morgan, illustrated by Suzanne Carpenter, Pont.

A longer poem might be read. Here is one of my own, which I have used with young children. Published by Child's Play International, the sequel, *Our Cat Cuddles*, comes with a story sack containing cat puppets, games and flash cards:

OUR DOG TINY

Mum and Dad said one day:

> *Would you like a puppy dog?*
> *We could get one from the RSPCA.*

I said:

> *I'd like a big dog, a barking dog,*
> *A bouncy, black and white dog.*

Mum said:

> *I'd like a floppy dog, a friendly dog,*
> *A fluffy, sit-on-your-knee dog.*

Dad said:

> *I'd like a mean dog, a lean dog,*
> *A growling, catch-a-thief dog.*

Elizabeth said:

> *I don't mind, whatever kind,*
> *Will be all right for me.*

At the pound we found
Lots and lots of dogs around.

I said:

> *I'd like a big dog, a barking dog,*
> *A bouncy, black and white dog.*

The Keeper said:

> *We've got fun dogs, gun dogs,*
> *Scotty dogs, spotty dogs,*
> *Snoopy dogs, droopy dogs,*
> *Leaping dogs, sleeping dogs,*
> *Hairy dogs, scary dogs,*
> *Even acrobatic dogs.*

Mum said:

> *I'd like a floppy dog, a friendly dog,*
> *A fluffy, sit-on-your-knee dog.*

The Keeper said:

> *We've got fat dogs, flat dogs,*
> *Shaggy dogs, scraggy dogs,*
> *Small dogs, tall dogs,*
> *Tubby dogs, chubby dogs,*
> *Skinny dogs, mini dogs,*
> *Even currant pudding dogs.*

Dad said:

> *I'd like a mean dog, a lean dog,*
> *A growling, catch-a-thief dog.*

The Keeper said:

> *We've got loud dogs, proud dogs,*
> *Rough dogs, tough dogs,*
> *Happy dogs, snappy dogs,*
> *Mad dogs, bad dogs,*
> *Collie dogs, jolly dogs,*
> *Even multi-coloured dogs.*

Elizabeth said:

> *I don't mind, whatever kind,*
> *Will be all right for me.*

We walked and walked
Around the pound,
And peered in every cage we found,
Until at last we all agreed
Upon a mongrel dog, a mop-rag dog,
A little bag of bones dog.

We named him Tiny and we took him home.
Since then he's grown and grown and grown and grown.

Dad says:

> *It chews the bumper on my car*
> *And rests its head on the breakfast bar.*

Mum says:

> *Its growl is like an express train*
> *The noise will drive me quite insane.*

I say:

> *With giant tusks and iron jaw*
> *It's crunched and munched my bedroom door.*

I don't care, said little Liz,
I like him just the way he is.
His tail is white, his paws are black,
Red bristles sprout along his back.
His eyes are of the palest green,
With the longest lashes you've ever seen.
One ear sticks up, the other down,
One ear is grey, the other brown.
I really think it is a shame
That lots of dogs all look the same.
Ours is as different as can be
And Tiny is the dog for me!

(© Gervase Phinn, first published in *Got You, Pirate!*,
compiled by John Foster, (Oxford University Press, 1994))

A favourite poem for performing with older infants and juniors is the traditional verse 'The Hairy Toe'. It is great fun to read and the children need little encouragement to join in with the eerie chorus in a ghostly tone. It is not for the faint of heart.

THE HAIRY TOE!

There was an old woman
Who went out to pick beans,
And she found a hairy toe.
She took it home with her,
And then she went to bed.
The wind began to moan,
And the stairs began to groan,
And far away
She heard a voice a-calling:

Oh, where's my hair-r-r-r-y To-o-oe?
Who has got my hair-r-r-r-y To-o-oe?

The old woman hid beneath the sheets,
And pulled the blankets tightly round her head.
The wind began to moan,
And the stairs began to groan.
Something was trying to get in,
And was at the window,
And not too far away
She heard a voice a-crying:

Oh, where's my hair-r-r-r-y To-o-oe?
Who has got my hair-r-r-r-y To-o-oe?

The old woman didn't move an inch,
And pulled the blankets even tighter round her head.
The wind began to moan,
And the stairs began to groan.
There was something at her door.
It crept across her floor,
And very close
She heard a voice a-whispering:

Oh, where's my hair-r-r-r-y To-o-oe?
Who has got my hair-r-r-r-y To-o-oe?

YOU'VE GOT IT!

There is an enormous range of rich, colourful and appropriate poetry collections available for young children: playground chants, nursery rhymes, simple counting rhymes, choral verse and jingles. In addition to these rhyming poems children should be introduced to non-rhyming verse at an early stage and come to appreciate that not all poetry rhymes. The recommended collections at the end of the book include poems which are witty, sad, lively, moving, magical, arresting and clever—many of which do not rhyme.

Chapter 3
Writing Poetry with Infants

Some of the best and most lasting effects of English teaching have come from the simultaneous encounter of teacher, pupil and text.

Bullock Revisited: A Discussion Paper by HMI, HMSO

Small children who may not possess the writing skills to work independently might be encouraged to work collaboratively on their poems, helped and supported by a sensitive teacher. They can be given a suggested pattern or framework for their writing and offered some rules to help get them started. A group of six and seven years olds sitting informally in the Home Corner talked generally about a small selection of stuffed animals and puppets which I had taken into school. The creatures included a mole, badger, fox cub, rabbit, squirrel, hedgehog and dormouse. At two further 'talk' sessions I read some poems and short descriptive extracts from stories which featured these animals. These included 'Mole', 'Squirrel', 'Shrew', 'Donkey' and 'Snail' by Ted Hughes (recently republished in *Ted Hughes: Collected Poems for Children*, illustrated by Raymond Briggs, Faber & Faber) and 'To a Squirrel at Kye-na-no' by W. B. Yeats from *The Collected Poems of W. B. Yeats*, Macmillan.

There are a wealth of short descriptive poems about animals in:

- *The Puffin Book of Fantastic First Poems*, edited by June Crebbin, Puffin.

- *Jumping the Waves: Sglod's Favourite Poems* by Ruth Morgan, illustrated by Suzanne Carpenter, Pont.

- *The Ring of Words: An Anthology of Poems for Children*, edited by Roger McGough, Faber & Faber.

- *Short Poems: A Book of Very Short Poems*, collected by Michael Harrison, Oxford University Press

- *Animal Poems*, compiled by Jennifer Curry, Scholastic.

We looked at each animal in turn and talked about the colours, shapes, features and anything the children wished to raise. I listed parts of the dormouse's body on the whiteboard:

eyes

ears

nose

mouth

tail

fur

The children suggested adjectives to add some description:

black round	eyes
soft flappy	ears
wet little	nose
small whiskery	mouth
thin pink	tail
soft brown	fur

Comparisons were then suggested. We decided together which ones we liked the best and from the discussions emerged our class poem:

DORMOUSE

Black, round eyes like shiny beads,
Soft, flappy ear like a crumpled purse,
Wet, little nose like sticky tar,
Small, whiskery mouth like a tiny cave,
Thin, pink tail like a lazy worm,
Soft, brown fur like a carpet.

The children, working in pairs, helped and supported by the teacher, produced some detailed descriptive verse based on this approach. Here are four examples

MOLE

Fat, black body like an old glove,
Shiny fur as soft as silk,
Sharp, little nose like an ice cream cone,
Big, flat paws like pink spades,
Eyes that cannot see.

(Carlie and Ruth)

BADGER

Bristly fur like a doormat,
Fat, round body like a dog's,
Long, sharp teeth like icicles,
Glistening eyes like marbles,
Black and white in the night.

(Ben and Daniel)

RABBIT

Big, big eyes as round as the moon,
Soft, soft fur as grey as the mist,
White whiskers like bits of cotton,
Round, little tail as white as the sky.

(Jordan and James)

HEDGEHOG

Round, spiky body like a ball of spikes,
Crinkled pointed face like an old, old man,
Long, long whiskers like spiky grass,
A carpet of spines, a bristly brush.

(Tom and Claire)

Another approach is for the teacher to act as the scribe and the children to compose a class poem to which a refrain is added. For example, just before an infant school Harvest Festival the children wrote a class poem which they performed with great enthusiasm and confidence for parents on the day. The classroom was full of a variety of fruit and vegetables and this afforded a good opportunity to talk about the produce—the colours, smells, shapes, sizes and so on. I wrote a list of words on the blackboard to which children added some descriptions:

oranges	round and rubbery
apples	hard and red
bananas	bent and blotchy
pears	fat and juicy
potatoes	dusty and hard
cabbages	crunchy and green
carrots	pointed and smooth
onions	flaky and brown
beetroot	dark as the night

We went through each phrase to see if any rhymes appeared naturally or if children could suggest any. I added one of my own. The refrain was decided upon when Sophie, who had brought a large basket of vegetables, announced proudly that 'Everything grows in my Grandpa's garden'. We all thought this chorus would be ideal. Here is the finished poem:

GRANDPA'S GARDEN

Big fat onions, flaky and brown,
Cucumbers soft and green,
Knobbly potatoes, dusty and hard,
The biggest you have ever seen.

Everything grows in Grandpa's Garden,
Everything grows and grows!

Long, thin carrots pointed and smooth,
Beetroot smooth and red,
Celery long and crunchy and green,
Cabbages as big as your head.

Everything grows in Grandpa's Garden,
Everything grows and grows!

Apples hard and munchy to eat,
Pears so juicy and round,
Bananas soft and blotchy and bent,
The longest that can be found.

Everything grows in Grandpa's Garden,
  Everything grows and grows!

In talking about the poems they hear and read and in writing verse, older infants and juniors start to become more confident in attempting to use some poetic devices. They begin, quite naturally, to include similes, alliteration, repetition and vivid imagery into their writing and start experimenting with rhymes and refrains. In one infant school I worked with a group of seven year olds undertaking a history project. The children had been asked by their teacher to interview their grandparents about what life was like when they were young, to make some notes and carry out a little simple research. As part of the project I read a range of poems and stories about grannies and grandpas including:

- 'My Grannie' by June Crebbin in *The Puffin Book of Fantastic First Poems*, edited by June Crebbin, Puffin.

- 'My Grandpa' by Ian Souter, 'My Gran' by Moira Andrew, 'Grandma's Winter Warmer' by Mark Bones and 'Granny Granny Please Don't Comb My Hair' by Grace Nichols in *Family Poems*, compiled by Jennifer Curry, Scholastic.

The children were then asked to share their impressions, writing down all the things they could think of about their grandparents: what they look like, the things they say, any memories they have mentioned, if they have special names. A first draft was attempted and I intervened to make some suggestions, help with spellings and encourage the children to put some of their ideas into words. The children were then asked to write a poem beginning: *My Grannie ...* or *My Grandpa ...* The final polished poems were illustrated, photocopied and displayed alongside photographs and paintings. My favourites were 'My Grannie' by Ruth, 'My Grandpa' by Elizabeth and 'My Granddad' by Peter:

MY GRANNIE

My Grannie says I am a little chatterbox.
She says I talk ten to the dozen.

Chatter, Chatter, Chatter,
Natter, Natter, Natter.

My Grandpa says—Never mind poppet,
You take after your Grannie.

Chatter, Chatter, Chatter,
Natter, Natter, Natter.

She's the world champion talker.

MY GRANDDAD

Is tall and thin and bald and jolly
And when he laughs his face creases up
Like the wrinkles on a crumpled shirt

MY GRANDPA

My grandpa is old now.
His head is as bald as a hard-boiled egg,
But inside millions of things are going on.

My grandpa is old now.
But when he sneezes,
He blows the leaves off the trees.

My Grandpa is old now.
But when he walks,
His legs go snip-snap like a pair of scissors.

My Grandpa is old now.
But when he smiles,
The sun comes out and the birds sing.

My Grandpa is old now.
But when he sings,
He makes the cups wobble on the shelf.

My Grandpa is old now.
But he doesn't act his age.

In a junior class I used the same approach and Thomas and Nadine, aged eleven, produced some excellent poems:

GRANDDAD

My Granddad has got lots of wrinkles round his eyes.
He has really old glasses and wears his hat in the house.
He has hairs in his ears and up his nose but not much
on his head.
He sleeps a lot and he snores a lot,
And when he eats sweets he makes a funny noise.

My Granddad left school when he was very young.
He worked down the pit where it was dark and dusty,
And looked after the ponies that pulled the carts of coal.
On his watch chain he has a little miner's lamp
And inside his watch he keeps a picture of Grandma.

(Thomas)

MY GRANDPA

My Grandpa collects me from Brownies every
Friday night.
He collects my friend Rachel as well.
We sit in the back of the car and put our seat belts on.
He drives really slowly and he sings,
In a loud and growly voice,
And I get really embarrassed.
'Grandpa,' I tell him, when he's dropped Rachel off,
'Please don't sing! I wish you wouldn't sing.'
So the next week when he collected us from Brownies
He didn't sing, he just drove the car.
'Mr Harris,' Rachel said after a while.
'Will you sing. I like it.'

(Nadine)

Chapter 4
Some Starting Points for Poetry with Juniors

> Analysis, especially if it is applied too early, makes the poem into a problem instead of an experience. And if the beginner is unlucky, it may become a problem before it has ever been an experience.
>
> Edwin Muir, *The Estate of Poetry*

Poetry needs to be experienced before it is analysed and any classroom activity where teachers are looking with their pupils at a poem should bring the listener and the reader closer together and not come between them. I was fortunate in my teachers that they lifted poetry from the page, exposed me to a wide variety of verse and helped me to understand the techniques of writing poetry but they made the pleasure principle paramount. Some young people, when they come upon poems for their examinations, interrogate the text with the teacher in maximum pleasure-destroying detail and thus come to dislike verse and believe that all poems have some kind of hidden meanings. Enjoyment of a poem can be deepened by analysis but close study at an early age is not the way.

One way of encouraging children to discuss the verse they hear and read is to present them with a poem on the whiteboard or on a printed sheet. They are asked to read the poem quietly to themselves before the teacher reads it aloud. Then the children are asked to read the poem along with the teacher. A poem rarely comes to life in one or two readings.

The children then might be set a series of open-ended questions:

1 What in one sentence is the poem about?

2 What parts of the poem do you like and why?

3 What parts don't you understand?

4 Is there anything else you wish to say about the poem?

They are then asked to write a short paragraph about the poem using their answers as prompts. Here is one response from Jonathan to the anonymous poem 'I Asked a Little Boy'.

I ASKED A LITTLE BOY

I asked a little boy who cannot see,
'And what is colour like?'
'Why green,' said he,
'Is like the rustle when the wind blows through
The forest; running water, that is blue;
And red is like a trumpet sound; and pink
Is like the smell of roses; and I think
That purple must be like a thunderstorm;
And yellow is like something soft and warm;
And white is a pleasant stillness when you lie
And dream.'

> 'The blind boy can't see things around him but imagines what colours sound and smell and feel like. I like the pictures that come into your head when you read this poem. I think purple is a dark and thundery colour and white is clean and smells nice like sheets on a bed. Yellow is like custard, soft and warm. This boy probably used to be able to see and remembers.'

> (Jonathan)

Ellie, an eight year old, responded to my poem 'A Trip to the Zoo':

A TRIP TO THE ZOO

Please, don't bring me back to the zoo,
No, don't bring me back to the zoo.
The trumpeting elephant looks really mad,
The old hippopotamus terribly sad,
As I said to my mum and I said to my dad,
'Please, don't bring me back to the zoo.'

Please, don't bring me back to the zoo,
No, don't bring me back to the zoo.
The bored looking tiger gnaws on a bone,
The poor old gorilla sits all on his own,
As I said to my parents: 'Oh, can I go home?
Please, don't bring me back to the zoo.'

Please, don't bring me back to the zoo,
No, don't bring me back to the zoo.
The chimps in their cages look terribly glum,
The wolves in their pens have nowhere to run,
As I said to my dad and I said to my mum,
'Please, don't bring me back to the zoo.'

(Published in *Don't Tell the Teacher*
by Gervase Phinn, Puffin)

'The poem is about a girl going to the zoo with her parents but she doesn't enjoy the trip. When children go to the zoo they like to see all the animals but this person doesn't because she feels sorry for them. They look so sad and bored. She thinks it is cruel to keep these wild animals locked up in cages and stared at by people. She makes us think about whether it is right to have zoos. I like the rhythm of this poem, it's catchy and I like the way she repeats the last two lines. '

(Ellie)

Teachers might like to try this technique with older children using two of my poems:

MISSING GRANDDAD

My Gran smells of lavender soap
And has a face full of wrinkles,
And eyes like small black shining beads.
Her hair is like silver thread
And her hands are as soft as a bed of feathers,
And when she's with my Mum, she talks a lot.

My Gran uses a tea bag three times,
And saves bits of soap in a jar,
And collects old newspapers and plastic bags,
And rubber bands and safety pins.
'Waste not, want not,' she says,
And when I visit, she laughs a lot.

My Gran wears thick brown stockings
And slippers with holes in
And a coloured scarf with a little silver brooch.
She keeps a photo of Granddad
On the old brown dresser,
And when she's alone, I think she cries a lot.

FUN AND GAMES

I hate football.
We have to line up on the field
While the two best players in the school,
Champions of the school team,
Martin Biggadyke and Barry Marshall,
Choose us one by one.
I wait, shivering in my shorts,
Looking clumsy and gangly and cold,
One of the dregs,
The last to be picked.
'Get in goal, Fatty Four Eyes!'
Orders Martin Biggadyke,
Poking me in the chest,
'And don't let any goals in, see,
Or you're dead!'
I stand there between the posts,
Before the net,
Shivering and afraid,
Counting the seconds
And praying for the end of the lesson.

From these open-ended questions the teacher might look a little more closely at the poems and introduce older children to some of the tools that poets employ to create an effect and to encourage their listeners to think:

Rhythm

Rhyme

Alliteration

Metaphor

Simile

Onomatopoeia

Repetition

Imagery

Tone of voice

Atmosphere and mood

Emphasis

Pace

In writing their own poems children may find these techniques useful and try to use them.

A simple starting point for junior children with little confidence is a strategy which involves reorganising, completing or adding to pieces of existing text. The DARTS (Directed Activities Related to Texts) approaches are useful in encouraging children to focus on aspects of the language and the structure of verse. A group of reluctant juniors with little experience of poetry were given a verse with single words and phrases omitted. They were asked, in groups of three, to discuss possible alternatives and fill in the spaces. I stressed that the poet's choice of words was not necessarily the right one and that there were several possible alternatives. The activity encouraged the children to engage actively with the poem and consider the verse in an interesting and creative way. The verses they considered were short poems of mine. Those who managed the first poem then tackled the second one, which proved much more demanding.

FARMGIRL

When she's collected the eggs
And ....,
Groomed the mare
And ....,
Filled the troughs
And ....,
Cooped the hens
And ....,
She then ....

FARMGIRL

When she's collected the eggs
And fed the chickens,
Groomed the mare
And cleaned the stalls,
Filled the troughs
And watered the pigs,
Cooped the hens
And walked the dog,
She then has an early night.

LAST IN THE QUEUE

When they gave out the ……………….,
I was last in the queue.
There were no ……………….,
……………….. or ……………….,
……………….. or ……………….,
……………….. or ……………….,
……………….. or ……………….,
……………….. or ……………….,
……………….. or ……………….,
There was only ………………..
The trouble is ………………..

LAST IN THE QUEUE

When they gave out the dinners,
I was last in the queue.
There were no carrots or cabbage,
Parsnips or peas,
Beans or beetroot,
Leeks or lettuce,
Cauliflower or celery,
Turnips or potatoes,
Apples or pears,
Oranges or bananas,
There was only pork, ham, chicken and corned beef.
The trouble is I'm a vegetarian.

The pupils were asked to compare their efforts and then the original versions were read:

FARMGIRL

When she's collected the eggs
And milked the cows,
Groomed the mare
And fed the sows,
Filled the troughs

And stacked the logs,
Cooped the hens
And penned the dog,
She then begins her homework.

LAST IN THE QUEUE

When they gave out the instruments at school,
I was last in the queue.
There were no trumpets or trombones,
French horns or flutes,
Violins or violas,
Clarinets or cornets,
Guitars or saxophones,
Euphoniums or bassoons,
Tubas or cellos,
Drums or piccolos or oboes.
There was only the double bass left for me.
The trouble is I'm four foot three.

Sequencing is another interesting activity which encourages children to discuss and examine a poem's structure. A Year 5 group was given a verse which had been jumbled up and the children were asked to place the lines in an order which made sense and which sounded interesting. Below are the original and the alternative version of a poem by Mark:

MY NAN

I like my Nan.
She's round and wrinkly and powdery
And smells of flowers and soap.
She's as comfy as a cushion to sit on.
When my mum shouts at me,
I go to my Nan.
She cuddles me and says,
"Never mind love,
Your mum was like that when she was a little girl
A real grumpybum!"

MY NAN

When my mum shouts at me,
I go to my Nan.
She's as comfy as a cushion to sit on,
She's round and wrinkly and powdery
And smells of flowers and soap.
I like my Nan.
She cuddles me and says,
"Your mum was like that when she was a little girl,
A real grumpybum!
Never mind love."

Another activity gives children the opportunity to create a poem from existing pieces of text. Year 6 children working in pairs wrote some short poems by rearranging phrases taken from short stories, newspapers and magazines. Here is a poem created from newspaper headlines (in italics) with a few conjunctions to help the sense.

A rough ride for the royals,
Who got *a kick in the right direction?*
Soap star in a lather
When *PM shows his mettle.*
Lawyers attack lenders
With *Mortars on the Move.*
Angry pensioners in fighting mood
When told, *There's no room at the inn.*
The barbarians of the blackboard
Start dealing the deadly blow
To *the world's youngest mother.*

Asking children to compose poems from names of people and places can also be productive and offer starting points. Here are two examples of my own with names taken from a local street map and an ordnance survey map of the Yorkshire Dales:

OUR TOWN

On Richard Road live John and Pat
And Parsley, their pet Persian cat.
On Lillian Street there's Mrs Bray
Who keeps her curtains closed all day.
The house on Austin Avenue
Belongs to Mr and Mrs Drew.
On Tennyson Drive Professor Rutter
Has pigeons nesting in his gutter.
On Ragsdale Rise just by the Park
Live James and Sally, Jane and Mark.
On Wharncliffe Crescent Mr Row
Lives in a little bungalow.
On Caedmon Close there's Dr Bates,
His house behind great iron gates.
On St Mary's cul-de-sac,
Lives the vicar, the Reverend Black.
A nosy neighbour with all the news
Is Mrs Mann of Mordlake Mews.
Down Balby Valley Boulevard
Lives Albert Potter, railway guard.
On Lilac Lane old Mrs Beecher
Displays a plate: 'Piano Teacher'.
On Tickhill Terrace live the Blasketts
With a house festooned with hanging baskets.
In the great dark villa on Harpers Way,
Are spooks and spectres—so they say.
On Markham Moor a mansion stands
The home of Lord and Lady Sands.
But the house I really like the best
Is much, much better than all the rest.
It's number 80 Nelson Crest … and I live there!

THE BIGGEST AND THE BEST

Buckdale Pike,
　Garrelgum Foss,
　　Hag Dike,
　　　Blaydike Moss,
　　　　Cocklee Fell,
　　　　　Dead Man's Cave,
　　　　　　Robin Hood's Well,
　　　　　　Giant's Grave,
　　　　　　　Kealcup Hill,
　　　　　　　Malham Tarn,
　　　　　　Bracken Gill,
　　　　　　　New Ing Barn,
　　　　　　　　Gordale Bridge,
　　　　　　　　Settle Sear,
　　　　　　　　　Winshill Ridge,
　　　　　　　　　Deepdale Carr,
　　　　　　　　　　Knuckle Bone Pasture,
　　　　　　　　　Ghaistrill's Strid,
　　　　　　　　　　Hawkswick Clowder,
　　　　　　　　　　Crutchin Gill Rigg.
In England, Ireland, Scotland, Wales, there's nowt as grand as t'Yorkshire Dales!

Older primary children, who possess the writing skills to work independently, might be encouraged to write free verse poems, using the selection of animals mentioned earlier, as stimuli. As with the infants we talked generally about the stuffed creatures which I supplemented with large coloured posters and pictures and various lifelike puppets. We talked about the shapes, colours and textures, focusing on certain features of the animals such as the teeth, eyes and mouth. I read some short non-fiction descriptions of the various creatures (mouse, chameleon, fox, rabbit, hamster and cat) using the bright and splendidly written board books produced by Child's Play International. I also read some poems and short descriptive extracts from stories which featured these animals. These included some poems of my own:

VISITOR

The day after they mowed the meadow
Behind our house,
A mouse
Appeared.
It poked its curious black-eyed whiskered face out
From behind the gas fire

And watched us watching television.
It joined us later for tea,
Nibbling the crumbs which fell from the table
Without a by-your-leave
And then returned to the dark warmth behind the
    gas fire.
Impudent rodent!
I have not the heart to set a trap.

CAT

I belong to no one—
Despite what they think.
Sleek am I and grey,
Soft-furred, jade-eyed,
Pink-tongued and whiskered,
Purring softly, stretching lazily.
Such a domesticated cat, they say.
Stroke me if you will.
Pet me,
Feed me,
But do not try and train me.
I belong to no one.
In this heart of mine
There burns the spirit of a savage blood.

PUSSY CAT

I am not your fat cat, snoozing-on-the-lap cat, shiny
    black as jet.
I am not your lazy, fluffy, softly purring, milky
    whiskered pet.
I am the killer cat, the night cat, the pouncing, scratch
    and biter,
The jade-eyed, catch-a-rat cat, a furry feline fighter.

LIZZIE'S HAMSTER

When we found Timmy,
Lizzie's hamster,
Curled up in the corner of his cage,
Lifeless and cold,
Our next-door-neighbour,
Mrs Gomersall,
Said:
'Are you sure he's dead?
Let me look.
Hamsters sleep deeply when it's winter.'

When she cradled Timmy,
Lizzie's hamster,
In her warm and wrinkled hands,
And stroked his little body,
Our next-door-neighbour,
Mrs Gomersall
Said:
'He's not dead!
See him stir.
Your hamster, he was sleeping deeply.'

When we popped Timmy,
Lizzie's hamster,
Back in his cage
Amongst the straw,
Our next-door-neighbour,
Mrs Gomersall,
Said:
'All he wanted
Was a little extra love and warmth—
Like all of us, really.'

A Year 5 class produced some excellent pieces of verse, such as the two below by Paul and Shania, which we displayed alongside the photographs on the classroom wall:

FOX

He stands on the wall
Watching,
Sharp-nosed, with his red bushy tail
And shining eyes like coloured beads.

He doesn't move,
Just watches,
Then he sniffs the air
And jumps lightly down
On the grass
And walks slowly away.

BEN

Ours is a scruffy dog,
A big, soft, fat, slobbering, fluffy dog.
He plods about the house
Then flops on the floor
And sighs.
Big brown paws,
Big brown eyes,
He's too lazy to even wag his tail!

BADGER

When the wood is silent,
When it's dark and still,
When there is no wind, no singing birds,
Then there is a movement in the grass,
A rustling and a crackling of twigs.
The badger is about,
Black and white,
Fat round bodied,
Sharp clawed,
He roams his forest home.

Chapter 5
Miniature Poems

A poet is a man speaking to men, of his and their condition, in language which consists of the best words in the best order, language used with the greatest possible inclusiveness and power.

Samuel Taylor Coleridge in *The Self as Mind: Vision and Identity in Wordsworth, Coleridge, and Keats* by Charles J. Rzepka

Poets, like artists, look carefully at their subjects, then select the very best words to describe them. Children might be encouraged to write miniature word pictures to try to capture in a few lines an image of the sea or the stars, an old man or a child, a mood or feeling, a celebration or a disaster. In *Short Poems: A Book of Very Short Poems* collected by Michael Harrison, Oxford University Press, are many examples of very short poems which offer excellent models for the children's own efforts.

Here are six miniature poems written by pupils aged ten and eleven:

ICICLES

Dangling daggers,
Slippery spikes,
Icy horns,
Winter's fangs.

(Elizabeth)

FOREST

Tall firs,
Sharp spears,
Like pointed pencils
They puncture the sky.

(Becky)

TRAFFIC

Huffing, puffing
Coughing, growling,
Chuddering, juddering—
Cars in a queue, lorries in a line.

(Daniel)

SCISSORS

Shiny slicers,
Silver snippers,
Snip-snap, snip-snap,
Like the legs of a dangerous dancer.

(Claire)

SEA SHELLS

Smooth and white like icing sugar,
Hard and yellow like old toenails,
Shiny and pink like sweets,
Round and black like eyeballs.

(James)

HAMSTER

Little furry ball,
Hiding in the straw,
Nibbling, scratching,
All the day.

(Kirstie)

Chapter 6
Patterned Poems

Poetry is the shortest way of saying things.
It also looks nicer on the page than prose.
It gives room to think and dream.

John Betjeman

Children might be encouraged to try a miniature word picture which follows a fixed pattern. In the following collections there is a range of carefully structured poetry: haiku, tanka, cinquain and diamont. Children like reading them and enjoy the challenge of writing their own.

The following collections contain some varied patterned poems:

* *Crack Another Yolk and Other Word Play Poems*, compiled by John Foster, Oxford University Press.

* *This Poem Doesn't Rhyme*, edited by Gerard Benson, Viking.

* *Cat Among the Pigeons* by Kit Wright, illustrated by Posy Simmonds, Puffin.

* *The Hat* by Carol Ann Duffy, Faber & Faber.

* *Wicked World!* by Benjamin Zephaniah, Puffin.

The syllable poem

As a preparation for the rhythmic precision of the haiku children might be asked to write a poem in which the number of syllables increases in progression from 1 to 5 and then back to 1. Here are two syllable poems by Year 6 pupils:

MISTY

Fat.
Fierce faced.
Amber eyed.
Purring gently.
Soft as a silk scarf.
Warm as a fire.
Breathing slowly.
Curved clawed.
Cat.

(Megan)

HOME

House.
Red brick.
Old oak door.
Greasy grey slate roof.
Gurgling gutters.
Wide-eyed windows.
Black chimney.
Warm fire.
Home.

(Jonathan)

The haiku

Traditionally this is a seasonal Japanese poem of three lines usually of 17 syllables:

Line 1: Setting of the scene (5 syllables)

Line 2: Embodies some action (7 syllables)

Line 3: Relates to or reflects the first two lines (5 syllables)

The haiku is a good way of getting children to write poetry for it is a verse form which is short, expresses an apparently simple idea (although often says something profound) and gives a clear structure to follow. Because it is often a free verse poem it does not distract the writer who often struggles to find a rhyme. Furthermore it is short enough to allow for quick revising and redrafting.

The following haiku were written by Year 6 children working on a project which focused on weather:

SPRING

Still water. White yachts
Stand like picnic sandwiches
On the quiet lake.

(Claire)

SUMMER

Hot day. Burning sun
Dries the soil to yellow dust
And toasts the pavements.

(Marcus)

AUTUMN

Strong wind. Whips up leaves,
Blows the washing off the line
And roars with pleasure.

(Oliver)

WINTER

Rough sea. Seagulls twirl
Like paper in the wind
Above the water.

(Simone)

The senryu

Named after the eighteenth century Japanese poet, Karai Senryu, this type of three-line verse is similar in form to the haiku. Like the haiku it often has a seasonal reference but it is different in that the senryu disregards the rigid rules of three lines with 5, 7 and 5 syllables and is more intentionally humorous in content.

The following amusing, short, sharp senryu were written by Year 6 children:

SUMMER

When the sun shines
And birds sing in the summer trees
I stay in bed.

(Ben)

BABY

'Isn't he lovely?'
Everybody said about my baby brother.
Just to be awkward I say, 'No!'

(Emma)

BEDROOM

Your bedroom's tidy at last.
My mother looks pleased.
But everything's under the bed.

(Anne-Marie)

MY SISTER

'I'll only be a minute!'
My sister shouting from the bathroom.
Sixty minutes later …

(Reece)

EXAM

I love exams
I really do.
And I tell lies as well.

(Devon)

MY DAD

'What did I just say?'
Shouts my Dad.
I think his memory must be going.

(Matthew)

The tanka

Another Japanese form of verse is the tanka, composed of five lines of 31 syllables. As with the haiku, traditionally the theme centres on lyrical subjects of nature, love and loss and there is often a quick turn at the end of the poem. It follows a particular pattern:

Line 1: (5 syllables)

Line 2: (7 syllables)

Line 3: (5 syllables)

Line 4: (7 syllables)

Line 5: (7 syllables)

Here are four verses composed by Year 6 pupils:

OLD HOUSE

Old house in winter,
Dark and cold and full of dust,
Rotten window frames,
Leaking roof and rising damp,
The home of spooks and spectres.

(Ben)

SPRING

Spring in the forest,
Buds bursting from the dark trees,
Bushes thick and green,
A carpet of bluebells bright,
And hawthorns blossom.

(Rahila)

BEACH

The beach in summer.
Brassy sun burning bodies,
A calm sea lapping,
Bathing beauties berry brown,
Old ladies snooze in deckchairs.

(Karl)

The cinquain

Another miniature five-line poem which describes something in small detail or tells of a simple experience is the cinquain. Its lines follow a particular pattern:

Line 1: The topic (2 syllables)

Line 2: Describes the topic (4 syllables)

Line 3: Expresses some action (6 syllables)

Line 4: Expresses a feeling or makes a statement (8 syllables)

Line 5: Sums up the topic (2 syllables)

Here are three which I wrote and have used with children in Years 5 and 6:

OLD HOUSE

Old house,
So dark, so cold,
A musty smell of mould,
And giant shivering shadows
Waiting.
A light
Under the door.
A whispering inside.
I run back up the stairs in fright
Phantoms.

BEANSTALK

Beanstalk
Reaches skywards,
Writhes like a giant snake
And leads to untold riches and …
The OGRE!

The following cinquains were written by eleven year olds

SCHOOL

School—
Crowded corridors,
Silent, endless lessons,
Long hours of listening.
Boredom.

STATION

Station—
Smoky black,
Round ribbed roof,
Smell of oily trains,
Mystery.

DENTIST

Dentist—
Bright eyes,
Peering, probing, prodding,
Testing his drill,
Terror!

FOX

Fox—
Red robber,
Sneaking, stalking, stealing,
Hiding from the Hunt,
Cunning.

The diamont

A more demanding and difficult poem to write is the diamont, a seven-line poem written in the shape of a diamond and which contains a contrast of ideas or descriptions. It follows this pattern:

Line 1: The topic (1 word)

Line 2: Describes the topic (2 words)

Line 3: Expresses some action (3 words)

Line 4: Relates to the topic (4 words)

Line 5: Action words about the opposite of the topic (3 words)

Line 6: Describes the opposite of the topic (2 words)

Line 7: Is the opposite of the topic (1 word)

Before attempting their own cinquain poems children might be given a series of contrasting ideas or opposites to think about and discuss:

YOUNG	and	OLD
FAST	and	SLOW
DARK	and	LIGHT
SUMMER	and	WINTER
WET	and	DRY
HOT	and	COLD
RICH	and	POOR
BIG	and	SMALL
HIGH	and	LOW
HEAVY	and	LIGHT

The following poems were written by Year 6 pupils:

LATE HOME

Mum—
Quiet, concerned,
Cooking, cleaning, coping.
Waiting, wondering, worrying, watching.
Sitting, snoring, sleeping,
Dozing, dreaming,
—Dad.

(Rebecca)

RAGS TO RICHES

Millionaire!
Money Man.
Power, position,
Stocks, shares, banking, business.
Hopeless, helpless, homeless,
Poor Man.
Down-and-Out.

(Robert)

DAY & NIGHT

Morning.
Bright light.
Waking, stretching, yawning.
Clear, fresh, sunny, warm.
Dark, cold, silent.
Pitch black.
Evening.

(Sarah)

WORK & PLAY

School.
Hard work.
Writing, reading,
English, Maths, Geography, Craft.
Laughing, relaxing, playing,
All day.
Holidays!

(Simon)

Chapter 7
Limericks

Poetry is a popular living art and the pleasures of rhythm and rhyme are part of common life.

Gerard Benson, Judith Chernaik and Cicely Herbert,
Poems on the Underground

Limericks are short, amusing and witty verses of five lines which follow a fixed pattern:

Line 1: Rhymes with second and fifth line (8 or 9 syllables)

Line 2: Rhymes with first and fifth line (8 or 9 syllables)

Line 3: Rhymes with fourth line (5 or 6 syllables)

Line 4: Rhymes with third line (5 or 6 syllables)

Line 5: Rhymes with first and second line (8 or 9 syllables)

Here are a few of my favourite anonymously written ones:

THERE WAS AN OLD MAN OF PERU

There was an old man of Peru,
Who dreamt he was eating his shoe.
He awoke in the night
In a terrible plight,
And found it was perfectly true.

THERE WAS A YOUNG MAN FROM BENGAL

There was a young man from Bengal
Who went to fancy dress ball.
He thought he would risk it
And go as a biscuit,
But a dog ate him up in the hall.

THERE WAS AN OLD MAN FROM NANTUCKET

There was an old man from Nantucket
Who kept all his cash in a bucket.
His daughter, named Nan,
Ran away with a man,
And as for the bucket, Nan took it.

THERE WAS A YOUNG MAN FROM JAPAN

There was a young man from Japan
Who wrote verses that never would scan.
When they said, 'But the thing
Doesn't go with a swing,'
He said, 'Yes, but I always like to get as
many words into the last line as I possibly can.'

A DENTIST NAMED ARCHIBALD MOSS

A dentist named Archibald Moss
Fell in love with the pretty Miss Ross.
Since he held in abhorrence
Her name, which was Florence,
He renamed her, his dear dental Floss.

THERE WAS YOUNG MAN OF ST BEES

There was a young man of St Bees
Who was stung on the arm by a wasp.
When they said, 'Did it hurt?'
He replied, 'No, it doesn't.
It's a good job it wasn't a hornet.'

THERE WAS AN OLD MAN OF BLACKHEATH

There was an old man of Blackheath
Who sat on his set of false teeth.
Said he, with a start,
'Oh, Lord, bless my heart!
I have bitten myself underneath!'

Here are three of mine:

THERE WAS AN OLD TEACHER CALLED BLEWITT

There was an old teacher called Blewitt,
Who was clever, and oh, how he knew it.
'Pay attention!' he roared,
'The work's on the board,
Take a look and then I'll go through it!'

THERE WAS AN EXPLORER CALLED BETTY

There was an explorer called Betty,
Who grew fat eating plates of spaghetti.
On a trek to Tibet,
She was caught in a net,
And displayed at the zoo as a Yeti.

MY GRANDMOTHER TRAVELLING IN SPAIN

My grandmother travelling in Spain,
Fell from a fast-moving train.
She bounced down the track,
And when she climbed back,
Exclaimed: 'Could I do that again?'

The following limericks were written by Year 5 children working in pairs. They had help from the teacher and a classroom assistant. A class collection was produced and illustrated by the children.

THERE WAS A YOUNG LADY CALLED BETTY

There was a young lady called Betty,
Who went for a swim near a jetty,
She swam in the dark,
And met a great shark,
And that was the end of poor Betty.

A NAUGHTY YOUNG SCHOOLBOY CALLED DENNIS

A naughty young schoolboy called Dennis,
Went on a school trip to Venice,
He pushed his best pal,
Into a canal,
Dennis was the menace of Venice.

I WAS FISHING ONE DAY IN A STREAM

I was fishing one day in a stream,
When I had a very strange dream,
When I took a look,
There on my hook,
Was a hundred and fifty pound bream.

A BULLY CALLED JOHN MORIATY

A bully called John Moriarty,
Tried to spoil a little girl's party.
She said, 'It's not fair!'
And threw him up in the air.
She was a black belt at karate.

A HORRIBLE TEACHER CALLED SAM

A horrible teacher called Sam,
Was a very violent man.
He shrieked and he shouted,
He thumped and he clouted,
Smack! Wallop! Crack! Bam!

Chapter 8
Clerihews

Poetry makes children feel happy, capable and creative.

Kenneth Koch, *Wishes, Lies and Dreams:*
Teaching Children to Write

A clerihew is a comic four-line verse, typically about a person named in one of the lines. Here are four of my own showing different rhyming patterns and a double clerihew:

Elizabeth said, 'I'm like a queen,	(a)
In my new dress of vivid green.'	(a)
Her brother Matt let out a scream,	(a)
'You're a wee bit early for Halloween!'	(a)

Our neighbour talking to my mum said:	(a)
'So I gave her a piece of my mind.'	(b)
To part with such a precious thing,	(c)
She must be very kind.	(b)

Mr Wilson wears a wig,	(a)
But for his head it's rather big.	(a)
In windy weather he was careless.	(b)
Now Mr Wilson's head is hairless.	(b)

'Do you want a smacked bottom my lad?'	(a)
Asked my father in threatening voice.	(b)
I'm not likely to say: 'Yes please, Dad.'	(a)
I don't think I have the choice!	(b)

(Published in *It Takes One to Know One*
by Gervase Phinn, Puffin)

CONVERSATION IN AN INFANT CLASS

'You look very deep in thought,'
The School Inspector said.
'Now tell me please, my little man,
What is going through your head?'

'Well, have you ever stopped to think?'
The little infant said,
'That when I'm twenty-one years old,
You'll probably be dead!'

(Published in *The Day Our Teacher Went Batty*
by Gervase Phinn, Puffin)

Chapter 9
Alphabet Poems

Poetry is playing with language and images.

Jennifer Dunn, Morag Styles and Nick Warburton, *In Tune with Yourself:
Children, Writing Poetry—A Handbook for Teachers*

Alphabet poems offer a clear structure for children and are fun to compose. A group of Year 6 pupils listened to a selection of alphabet poems which included 'The Alphabest' by Carol Ann Duffy in her collection *The Hat*, Faber & Faber, and '"A" Begins Another' by Julie Holder in *Crack Another Yolk and Other Word Play Poems*, compiled by John Foster, Oxford University Press.

Following some discussion, I asked the children, working in groups, to try their hand at writing an alphabet poem and offered some guidelines:

- Write the alphabet down the left hand side of a sheet of paper;

- Refer to the range of reference material available—dictionaries, telephone directories, word lists and a children's encyclopaedia;

- Decide on a subject—it could be: animals, pop groups, monsters, people's names, places, occupations;

- Your poems do not need to rhyme and difficult letters such as X can be left out;

- When the poem is completed make the first letter of each line big and colourful so it stands out.

Before the children started, I gave each group the beginning of an alphabet poem and asked the pupils to continue it. This was to give them a little practice before they attempted a complete one of their own.

ALPHABET POEM: OCCUPATIONS

A   is for an Actor who's big on the stage.
B   is for Baron in his big grey castle.
C   is for Conductor counting his change.
D   is for the Doctor diagnosing.
E   is for Emperor who has everything.
F   is for Friar, friendly old monk.
G   is for gardener gathering his greens.

ALPHABET POEM: ANIMALS

Angry Aardvarks ate all the apples.
Brave bulls butted the bandits.
Cowardly cats cried in the custard.
Dangerous dogs danced in the drains.
Elegant elephants expanded every day.
Fierce furry ferrets found few friends.
Ghastly ganders got greedy in Greece.

I read two of my own alphabet poems explaining to the children the research I undertook, the drafting and refining process.

A MONSTER ALPHABET

A   is for ALIEN, arriving by air,
B   is for BASILISK, with the deadliest stare.
C   is for CYCLOPS, he's only one eye,
D   is for DRAGON, he'll light up the sky.
E   is for EXTRATERRESTRIAL CREATURES,
F   is for FRANKENSTEIN of the frightening features.
G   is for GRIFFIN, a lion with a beak,
H   is for HYDRA, the many-headed freak.
I   is for the INVISIBLE CREATURES of night,
J   is for JACK-O-LANTERN, that bright little sprite.
K   is for KELPIE with the great snapping teeth,
L   is for LOCH NESS and the MONSTER beneath.
M   is for MERMAID who appears from the deep,
N   is for NIGHTMARE that troubles your sleep.
O   is for the OPERA PHANTOM who sings,

P   is for PHOENIX with its fiery wings.

Q   is for QUASIMODO, who swings from his bell,

R   is for ROC the great bird of Hell.

S   is for SANDMAN, he'll steal every dream,

T   is for TROLL, 'neath the bridge and the stream.

U   is for UNICORN, with the long horn of gold,

V   is for VAMPIRE in his tomb dark and cold.

W   is for WEREWOLF who howls 'neath the sky,

X   is for XANTHUS, the horse that can fly.

Y   is for YETI, that abominable beast,

Z   is for ZOMBIE—the last but not least.

(Published in *Family Phantoms* by Gervase Phinn, Puffin)

MR FISHER'S THOUGHTS ON MARKING THE SCHOOL REGISTER

Angela Anchovy (she's a shy little girl and no mistake),

Barry Barracuda (gets his teeth into everything he does),

Colin Carp (complains all the time),

Daphne Dover-Sole (thinks she's the only one in the class),

Eric Eel (slippery customer that one),

Felicity Flounder (way out of her depth in class),

Gordon Grayling (likeable but lacklustre),

Harry Haddock (caught him smoking by the bike sheds),

Ian Icefish (a cool customer),

Jeremy John Dory (pushy parents),

Katy Kipper (falls asleep in class),

Leonard Lamprey (latches onto others),

Martin Mullet (just look at his hair),

Naomi Nurse-Fish (gentle natured creature),

Oliver Oilfish (another slippery individual),

Pricilla Perch (prickly member of the school),

Quentin Queenfish (thinks he's superior),

Rachel Roach (reliable girl),

Samantha Salmon (that pink lipstick will have to go),

Teresa Trout (old for her age),

Ursula Unicorn-Fish (such a bashful child),

Vincent Viper-Fish (vicious boy),

William Whiting (pale faced child),

Xavier X-Ray-Fish (eyes in the back of his head),

Yolanda Yellowtail (frightened little girl),

Zeberdee Sander (bottom of the school).

Becky and Claire produced a very clever and amusing alphabet poem:

OUR ALPHABETICAL CLASS

Angela is top in art,
Ben's best at biology,
Carol's poems are really nice,
Danny's good at geography.
Elsa daydreams all the day,
Frank is football crazy,
Grace is ace at outdoor games,
Hyacinth is lazy.
Ian—he's computer mad,
Janice likes to swim,
Karl is always first at school,
Lynn she loves the gym.
Mandy's science is really good,
Nicola's best in maths,
Oliver plays the violin,
Paula—she acts daft.
Quentin's homework's never done,
Ruth's a super singer,
Simon's in the football team,
Tom is a right-winger.
Ursula likes to write and write,
Veronica plays the fool,
Wendy loves to read a book,
Xavier thinks he's cool.
Yvonne she likes to cook and cook,
Zoë—she never ever goes to school.

Chapter 10
Acrostic Poems

Poetry comes from the conscious organisation of language in a form calculated to give pleasure and satisfaction in itself.

James Reeves

Acrostics are puzzle poems in which the beginning, middle or last letters of each line form a word vertically. Children enjoy creating acrostics; they offer a clear pattern and are fun to devise. A group of Year 6 pupils read a range of acrostic poems including 'Brother' and 'Sister' by Brian Merrick in *Crack Another Yolk and Other Word Play Poems*, compiled by John Foster, Oxford University Press, and 'Steam Train' by June Crebbin in *The Crocodile is Coming!*, Walker Books.

A range of acrostic poems, written by secondary school pupils, were then discussed. These included:

BULLY

Big booted brute

Ugly face, leering and sneering.

Little pig eyes, shiny as beads,

Long eagle nose, sharp as a hook.

You have more hair than brains!

(Lesley)

FIRST BORN

Hear her first sharp cry

And see her;

Pink and panting,

Pouting little lips,

In mother's arms.

New arrival, tiny miracle,

Elf like,

Soft little bundle.

Ssshh.

(Jonathan)

Claire wrote 'Dog & Cat', Russell and William produced the clever and imaginative acrostic 'Skyscraper' and Julia and Terri the two verses 'Nessie' and 'Dragon'. 'Yeti' and 'Banshee' are my own.

DOG & CAT

Dangerous
Old
Grumbler.

Claws
And
Teeth.

SKYSCRAPER

Soaring high,
King of the sky.
You are the tallest,
Swaying in space.
Cloud-topped tower,
Rising from the ground
Above everything.
Perhaps one day
Everything will be
Reaching to the skies.

NESSIE

Night came.
Everyone was in bed
Sleeping,
Snoring.
In the loch
Enormous creatures swam.

DRAGON

Down in the forest
Roaring in his den
A fire-breathing creature
Gobbles up the men.
Only princes strong and brave
Never get eaten in his cave.

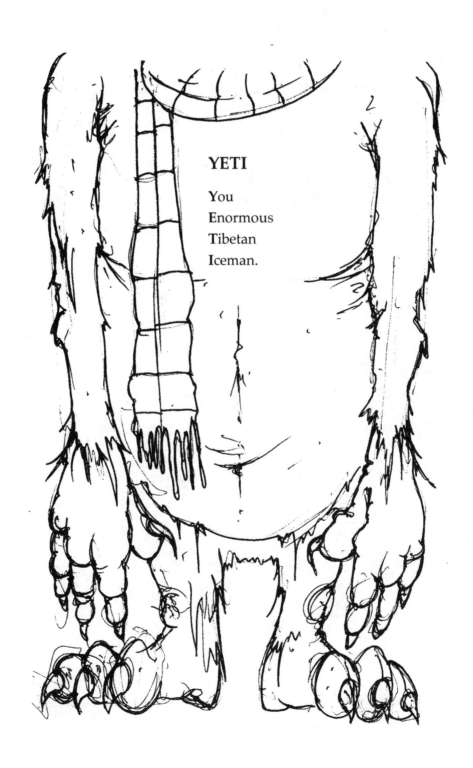

YETI

You
Enormous
Tibetan
Iceman.

BANSHEE

Bar the door,
And bolt the shutter
No one stir,
Speak or mutter.
Hark! Can you hear it,
Eerily howling,
Endlessly prowling?

(Published in *Family Phantoms* by Gervase Phinn, Puffin)

Chapter 11
Concrete Poems

The language of poetry is refinement, an organisation and selection of the best in human experience.

James Reeves

Concrete or shape poems (sometimes called calligrams) encourage children to use their imaginations and appreciate how the arrangement of the words on the page creates the impression of the chosen subject. Prior to writing their own, a group of Year 6 pupils looked at a range of shape poems which included 'Kite' by June Crebbin in *The Ring of Words: An Anthology of Poems for Children*, edited by Roger McGough, Faber & Faber, and 'Teardrop', 'Ball' and 'Vacuum Cleaner' in *Stars, Cars, Electric Guitars* by James Carter, Walker Books. There is a good selection of shape poems in the following collections:

- *Crack Another Yolk and Other Word Play Poems*, compiled by John Foster, Oxford University Press.

- *Jumping the Waves: Sglod's Favourite Poems* by Ruth Morgan, illustrated by Suzanne Carpenter, Pont.

- *My Dog Is a Carrot* by John Hegley, Walker Books.

- *The Crocodile is Coming!* by June Crebbin, illustrated by Mini Grey, Walker Books.

UPS AND DOWN

Up and down, up and down, on the escalator in the town,

Up **and** down, up and down, on the escalator in the town,

Up and **down**, up and down, on the escalator in the town,

Up and down, **up** and down, on the escalator in the town,

Up and down, up **and** down, on the escalator in the town,

Up and down, up and **down**, on the escalator in the town,

Up and down, up and down, **on** the escalator in the town,

Up and down, up and down, on **the** escalator in the town,

Up and down, up and down, on the **escalator** in the town,

Up and down, up and down, on the escalator **in** the town,

Up and down, up and down, on the escalator in **the** town,

Up and down, up and down, on the escalator in the **town**.

We looked at two of my poems and discussed the arrangement of the words on the page.

DOWNPOUR

It's:
  Raining,
    raining,
      soaking,
        spattering,
          flowing,
            flooding,
              pouring
Filling   down.
  gutters,
    gushing,
      spluttering,
        forming puddles
          through the
It's: town.
  Making
    all the rooftops oily
      black and shiny,
        wet and stark,
          running rivers
            down the windows,
It's: dreary, dismal,
  Raining,   cold and dark.
    raining,
      drenching,
        dousing,
          splashing,
            swamping,
Weeping,   pouring down,
  seeping,
    pounding,
      leaping,
        splattering,
          spitting—
            I might drown!

70

The children produced poems based on parts of the body (eyes, feet, nose), fruit (pine-apple, banana, pear, apple), animals (cat, elephant, giraffe), fish (shark, eel, jellyfish) and various shapes (star, diamond, crown, heart). Alice and Mark, taking the idea from Michael Gibbs's *Typewriter Poems*, produced four shape poems using the computer and based them on some well-known proverbs: 'All's well that ends well', 'He who laughs last, laughs longest', 'Birds of a feather flock together' and 'Every cloud has a silver lining':

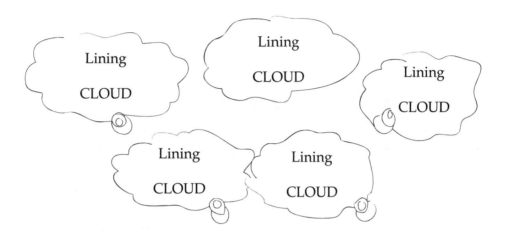

well
well
well
well
well
well
well
well
well
well
well

Laugh … Laugh … Laugh … Laugh … Laugh … Laugh … Laugh … Laugh … Laugh … Laugh … Laugh … Laugh … Laugh … Laugh … Laugh … Laugh … Laugh … Laugh … L a u g h.

BIRDSBIRDSBIRDS BIRDSBIRDSBIRDS BIRDSBIRDSBIRDS BIRDSBIRDSBIRDS
BIRDSBIRDSBIRDS
BIRDSBIRDSBIRDS
BIRDSBIRDS
BIRDS

Chapter 12
Riddles

Poetry is a matter of words. Poetry is a stringing together of words in a ripple and jingle and run of colours. Poetry is an interplay of images. Poetry is an iridescent suggestion of an idea. Poetry is all these things and still is something else.

D. H. Lawrence in *Introductions and Reviews*,
edited by N. H. Reeve and John Worthen

Riddles are words puzzles cleverly written and fun to solve. Here is a traditional riddle:

Four stiff standers,
Four dilly-danders,
Two lookers,
Two crookers
And a wig-wag.

As an introduction to riddles children might be asked to look at this anonymous poem which shows how words can have different meanings:

HAVE YOU EVER SEEN

Have you ever seen a sheet on a river bed?
Or a single hair on a hammer's head?
Has the foot of a mountain any toes?
And is there a pair of garden hose?

Does the needle ever wink its eye?
Why doesn't the wing of a building fly?
Can you tickle the ribs of a parasol?
Or open the trunk of a tree at all?

Are the teeth of rake ever going to bite?
Have the hands of a clock any left and right?
Can the garden plot be deep and dark?
And what is the sound of the birch's bark?

Here are three riddles of mine which I have used with older junior children:

A CLOSE COMPANION

As you sit all tense in the dentist's chair,
Eyes tightly closed, hands pressed together,
Listening to the whining drill—
I am there,
With you.

As you lay in bed in the shadowy dark,
And outside a cold wind rustles the leaves,
And branches scrape the window like claws—
I am there,
With you.

As you wade in the warm blue water,
Feeling the sandy sea bed soft beneath your feet,
And imagining what creature swims below—
I am there,
With you.

As you prepare to tell the angry teacher
Who sits glowering at his desk,
That you have not done your homework—
I am there,
With you.

I am the one who
Makes you tremble and sweat,
Makes your heart thump like a drum,
Makes your throat dry and your chest tight,
I am the one who fills your head with the most dreadful
   thoughts—
And you know my name.

(Published in *Don't Tell the Teacher*
by Gervase Phinn, Puffin)

74

WHAT AM I?

I gust and I bluster,
I rage and I rumble,
I shriek and I storm and I soar.
I whistle and waft
And cause the cold draught
As I breathe on the windows and under the door.
I rattle the branches
And rustle the grass.
I raise up the waves on the shore.
I eddy and whirl,
I twist and I twirl
The carpet of leaves on the ferny forest floor.

WHAT AM I?

It cannot be bought or borrowed
It cannot be stolen or sold
But this precious gift
When freely given
Is a pleasure to behold.
For it reassures the frightened,
It soothes those who are sad,
And comforts the dejected,
And makes the mournful glad.

It brightens up this weary world
And lightens up our life,
Brings sunshine to the shadows
At a time of pain and strife.

(For the answers to the riddles see overleaf)

In the following collections are a range of riddles, some of one line, others long, some easy to solve, others difficult, some over 900 years old and others modern:

- *100 Best Poems for Children*, edited by Roger McGough and illustrated by Sheila Moxley, Puffin.

- *The Ring of Words: An Anthology of Poems for Children*, edited by Roger McGough, Faber & Faber.

- *Crack Another Yolk and Other Word Play Poems*, compiled by John Foster, Oxford University Press.

Children might be encouraged to work in pairs to devise their own riddles using the following guidelines:

- Decide on the subject—it could be an object, place, animal or flower;

- Discuss and jot down the ideas that come into your head when you think about your chosen subject;

- Try to create a word picture or image of your subject in your mind;

- Decide whether your riddle is a one liner or a longer and more detailed puzzle;

- Try your riddle out on others in the class;

- Compile a class anthology or mount a wall display entitled—What Am I?

Below are six riddles written by Year 6 pupils:

Metal slider,
Noisy snake,
Smelly transporter,
Comfortable carrier,
Singing on the rails.

(Train)

They walk on me.
They beat me and drop things on me.
Nail me to the floor
And leave me to fade in the sunlight.

(Carpet)

Answers to riddles: Cow, Fear, Wind, Smile

I am a real square
Dry as dust,
Grey as a stone,
Paper thin and perforated.
I may be a square and full of holes,
But in hot water my flavour bursts,
For I am the quencher of thirsts.
What am I?

(Tea bag)

I've got a body but not a leg,
I've got a horn but not a head,
I have no foot but have a boot,
I can fire back but cannot shoot,
I have a bonnet, sometimes a hood,
I am made of metal and rubber and wood. What am I?

(Car)

I have a face but not a mouth,
I have hands but no arms,
I can stand but cannot sit,
And I go on for hours and hours.

(Grandfather clock)

I'm an icy blossom,
A tiny piece of frozen paper,
A cold white petal,
A winter pattern.

(Snowflake)

Chapter 13
Ballads

The purpose of poetry is not to inform but to inflame.

Vernon Scannell, How to Enjoy Poetry

A ballad is a simple and often quite lengthy poem which tells a story through dialogue and which is characterised by clear, direct language and a melodic refrain. The earliest narrative poems in English are the ballads, anonymously written and passed from generation to generation by word of mouth. Most ballads have a regular rhyme scheme of ABAB or AABB and a regular rhythm of 4, 3, 4, 3 beats to a verse of four lines. A good introduction to this verse form is a reading of 'Ballad' by W. H. Auden and 'The Sound Collector' by Roger McGough in *The Ring of Words: An Anthology of Poems for Children*, edited by Roger McGough, Faber & Faber.

Ballads, like the Anglo-Saxon epic poem *Beowulf,* are typical of this verse form and have a pounding rhythm and fast action. The evil Grendel has been killing and devouring Hrothgar's warriors for twelve long years. Then the mightiest and bravest warrior of them all, Beowulf, fights and kills the beast with his bare hands. The description of the battle in the lake between the super-hero Beowulf and Grendel, the monster's mother who seeks revenge, is guaranteed to hold any child's attention. It is interesting to compare the modern version of this classic ballad with the original Anglo-Saxon. Children will learn about the origins of our language and older ones might be encouraged to write some Anglo-Saxon verse themselves.

The Medieval ballad *Sir Gawain and the Green Knight* is another blood-stirring narrative poem, which offers an excellent springboard for art and display work and for drama.

Anonymous ballads such as 'Edward', 'Lord Randall', 'Sir Patrick Spens' and 'The Lambton Worm' really need to be performed. For older juniors extracts from some classic ballads—Robert Browning's 'The Pied Piper of Hamelin', Coleridge's 'The Rime of the Ancient Mariner', Tennyson's beautiful 'Morte d'Arthur' and the magical 'The Lady of Shalott', and Walter Scott's 'Lochinvar'—might be read and again offer varied possibilities for display and drama. 'The Highwayman' by Alfred Noyes is a must. The edition illustrated by Charles Keeping is outstanding. 'The Song of Hiawatha' by Henry Wadsworth Longfellow is another favourite. Children might be moved (as I was when I first read them) by the more sentimental ballads: Dorothea Hemans's 'The Boy Stood on the Burning Deck', 'Little Orphan Annie' and 'The Tiny Shroud'.

My ballad, 'The Mermaid', has the rhyme scheme of AABCCB and a regular rhythm to a verse of six lines.

THE MERMAID

'Twas an evening in December,
A night I well remember,
I was drinking in a tavern by the sea,
When I heard a mournful groaning,
A sad and sorry moaning,
'Twas coming from the table next to me.

I turned to face a seaman,
Though he looked more like a demon,
For his eyes were rolling wildly in his head.
He was light as any feather,
With a face as lined as leather,
And trembling lips, a savage shade of red.

'I was captain of a rigger!'
Cried the poor, pathetic figure,
'And what I tell thee stranger it be true.
One stormy day out sailing,
I heard a melancholy wailing,
Which carried o'er the ocean deep and blue.

'Twas not the cold wind in the sails,
Nor the cry of humpback whales,
'Twas not the creaking as the vessel pitched and rolled.
For the strange sound in my head,
Which filled my heart with dread,
'Twas like an angel weeping for lost souls.

By the cold sun's eerie light,
I then saw such a sight,
That I never shall forget—and that's no lie.
I near fainted with the shock,
For there upon a rock,
Sat a mermaid 'neath the cold December sky.

In all the places that I've been,
And all the beauty that I've seen,
She was a vision far beyond compare.
Her skin was marble smooth and white,
And her green eyes caught the light,
And lustrous was her soft and silky hair.

Now the salty tales of old,
That the ancient sailors told,
Said that if you look a mermaid in the eye,
You are doomed to spend your life,
With that mermaid as your wife,
And be with her until the day you die.

Oh, I heard the mermaid moan,
Oh, I heard her sigh and groan,
And I knew for sure the creature wanted me.
I could not resist her calling,
And very soon was falling,
Plunging headlong to the cold and friendless sea.

I smelt her weedy breath,
And her fingers cold as death,
As she clutched me in her watery embrace.
She would not let me go,
And she pulled me down below,
And kissed me, oh so gently on the face.

Then she sank beneath the waves,
And I was carried to her caves,
Filled with precious jewels and pearls and gold galore.
But all the treasure of the sea,
Is no earthly good to me,
For I am doomed to stay there evermore.

You think: Why is he here?
Well stranger, once a year,
I am allowed to come to shore one night,
To warn men such as thee,
Who sail upon the sea,
To avoid this accursed figure's plight.

And now I must away,
For the tide is in the bay,
And I hear so clear the mermaid's distant cry.
Do not think my tale absurd,
But believe me—every word—
And pity such a woeful man as I.

Oh, stranger heed my warning,
For the day will soon be dawning,
And I must now return beneath the sea.
So, if you're out a sailing
And hear a strange, enchanting wailing,
Stop your ears, for the mermaid's calling thee.'

Then before I could reply,
The seafarer gave a sigh,
And rolled his eyes and looked at me with dread.
I heard his mournful groaning,
His sad and sorry moaning,
And I saw him shake his old and weary head.

Then without one word more,
The figure shambled for the door,
Trembling in the candle's dying light,
And I was left alone,
Chilled to the very bone,
At the pitiful story I had heard that night.

I called the landlord from the bar.
'Tell me, who was that old tar,
Who sat with me this evening by the fire?'
The landlord answered: 'Who?
Why there was no one there but you.
And you've been talking to yourself for half an hour.'

The following ballads I have found work well in the classroom:

- 'The Pied Piper of Hamelin' by Robert Browning in *The Oxford Book of Story Poems*, Oxford University Press.

- 'The Highwayman' by Alfred Noyes in *The Oxford Book of Story Poems*, Oxford University Press.

- 'The Ballad of Birmingham' by Dudley Randall and 'A Smuggler's Song' by Rudyard Kipling in *I've Got a Poem for You: Poems to Perform*, collected by John Foster, illustrated by Belle Mellor, Oxford University Press.

A group of older juniors attempted some ballads. After hearing 'The Ballad of Johnny Shiner' by John Cunliffe and 'Lord Ullin's Daughter' by Thomas Campbell, read rather dramatically, they were asked to think about:

- subject

- rhyme scheme

- rhythm

- number of verses

- verse length

- choice of words

In small groups some pupils acted out the story using mime as well as their own words while another group prepared a dramatic reading and performed it with a partner. They were then asked to write a short ballad based on a story heard on the television or radio or read about in the newspapers. Here is a short ballad by one group:

THE BALLAD OF THE STRANDED CLASS

It happened in September of nineteen ninety three.
A class of children and their teacher were on a school trip to the sea.
They explored the dripping caves and they walked along the sand,
And they forgot about the time and soon were far from land.

The grey sea started getting rough, the winds began to blow,
The boats bobbed on the water and the seaweed swirled below,
The rock pools started filling up and the rain began to fall,
And the cliff rose from the sandy beach like a grey and towering wall.

The teacher started shouting and the children waved their hands,
And the icy ocean waters came rushing up the sands.
The little group were stranded on a dark and pebbly beach.
No one seemed to hear their cries for they were out of reach.

But a lighthouse keeper saw them from his tall and whitewashed tower,
And all were safe and sound again in less than half an hour.

Chapter 14
Cautionary Verse

Pupils should have opportunities to write poetry and to experiment with different layouts, rhymes, rhythms, verse structures and with all kinds of sound effects and verbal play.

English in the National Curriculum

Cautionary verses serve as a warning. They caution children not to be mean or selfish or cruel to animals, to behave themselves, eat what is given to them, not to complain and to be careful. These narrative poems were popular in Victorian times and were moral stories in verse intended to encourage children to be good and obedient. In all of them the recalcitrant child or cruel adult gets what he or she deserves.

Dr Heinrich Hoffmann's *Der Struwwelpeter* was the most popular, well-known and celebrated collection of cautionary verses in its time. Published in Frankfurt in 1845 it was translated into many languages and has been imitated, adapted and parodied over the years. These 'merry stories and funny pictures for children between three and six years old', as Dr Hoffmann termed them, are by turns macabre, pitiful and ridiculously amusing.

The verses include the story of Harriet who plays with matches and burns to death, and Conrad, the Little Suck-a-Thumb, who having been warned by his mother that if he doesn't desist from his nasty habit, the tailor will come with his great, sharp scissors and snip off his fingers. The disobedient Conrad continues to suck his thumb and gets a visit from the demon tailor. The accompanying graphic illustrations leave nothing to the imagination. Then there is Fritz, who is eaten by a wolf, cruel Frederick who 'killed the birds and broke the chairs and threw the kittens down the stairs' and who gets his just deserts and the cry-baby whose eyes eventually fall out. They are not poems for the delicately inclined but older juniors will relish ones like Augustus who refused to eat his soup and starved himself to death.

Augustus was a chubby lad;
Fat ruddy cheeks Augustus had;
And everybody saw with joy
The plump and hearty healthy boy.
He ate and drank as he was told,
And never let his soup get cold.

But one day, one cold winter's day,
He threw the bowl and spoon away.
'O take the nasty soup away!
I won't have any soup today:
I will not, will not eat my soup!
I will not eat it, no!'

Next day! Now look the picture shows,
How lank and lean Augustus grows!
Yet though he feels so weak and ill,
The naughty fellow cries out still:
'Not any soup for me I say!
O take the nasty soup away!
I will not, will not eat my soup!
I will not eat it, no!'

The third day comes. O what a sin!
To make himself so pale and thin.
Yet, when the soup is put on table,
He screams as loud as he is able:
'Not any soup for me, I say!
O take the nasty soup away!
I won't have any soup today!'

Look at him, now the fourth day's come!
He scarce outweighs a sugar-plum;
He's like a little bit of thread;
And on the fifth day he was—dead.

Hilaire Belloc is the undisputed master of the modern cautionary verse and his story of the disobedient Matilda, who played with fire, is a children's classic.

Cautionary verses are usually composed of rhyming couplets with four beats to the line. Using two of my own cautionary verses, which the children and I read together and discussed, I encouraged a class of older juniors to try one of their own.

CUTHBERT GREY

This is the tale of Cuthbert Grey,
Who liked near railway lines to play.
On the embankment he would lie
And watch the trains go thundering by.
He loved to see the engine's gleam
And hear the hissing of the steam.
He loved to hear the clickety-clack
Of train wheels travelling down the track.
Below the bridge he'd stand and stare
At white smoke billowing in the air.
He thought that it was such good fun

Beside the speeding the trains to run.
The engine driver shouted: 'Oi!
Get off the tracks you silly boy!
Can't you read the danger signs:
"Keep away from railway lines"?'
But Cuthbert, he just pulled a face
And all along the track he'd race.
He paid no heed to the driver's warning.
And then one sunny summer morning
Down the embankment Cuthbert leapt
And into the railway tunnel crept.
He thought that it would be a lark
To explore the tunnel, cold and dark.
He never heard the whistle scream,
He never saw the cloud of steam,
He never heard the driver shriek,
He never heard the train wheels screech.
Poor Cuthbert was not seen again.
Sadly he'd caught the London train.
Or perhaps it would be truer to say
That the London train caught Cuthbert Grey.

ICARUS

Icarus thought that he would fly
Like a seagull in the sky.
He made some wings with wood and tacks,
And stuck the lot with sealing wax.
Then, climbing to a cliff top high
He launched himself into the sky.
He soared and swooped without a care,
He flapped and fluttered through the air.
Then, on a current he was lifted
And upwards through the clouds he drifted.
He did not think it such good fun
When Icarus felt the fiery sun.
Its burning rays shone on his back,
And melted all the sealing wax.
You should have heard the dreadful yell,
As down to earth poor Icarus fell.
The moral of this tale is clear:
Make sure you have the proper gear
If you go flying way up high,
Like a seagull in the sky,
Or you like Icarus will descend
And come to such a sticky end.

Jon composed his cautionary verse with some help from the classroom assistant and a rhyming dictionary.

SILLY SALLY

Sally's mum was always saying
That she should watch the road while playing,
And keep away from caravans,
Buses, lorries, cars and vans,
To stay behind the garden wall
And not go near the road at all.
One day when playing with her ball,
She kicked it over the garden wall.

Down the road the ball it rolled
And Sal ignored what she'd been told,
To keep away from caravans,
Buses, lorries, cars and vans,
And stay behind the garden wall
And not go near the road at all.
Through the gate the girl she ran
And ended up beneath a van.
So, take extra care or like poor Sal
You'll end up in the hospital!

Here are some cautionary verses you light like to read to children:

• 'Matilda' by Hilaire Belloc, 'Kenneth' by Wendy Cope, 'The Lion and Albert' by Marriott Edgar and 'The Story of Little Suck-A-Thumb' by Dr Hoffmann in *100 Best Poems for Children*, edited by Roger McGough and illustrated by Sheila Moxley, Puffin.

• 'Icarus' by Peter Dixon in *The Tortoise Had a Mighty Roar*, Macmillan.

Chapter 15
Conversation Poems

Poems are jokes, lessons, speeches, complaints, boasts, hopes, dreams, rumours, insults, gossip, memories, lists. I see each poem I write, each poem I read, each poem I hear as part of a conversation.

Michael Rosen, *I See a Voice*, Thames

Children enjoy reading poems in twos and threes, lifting the verses from the page and performing them for others. There is a wide range of conversation poems about pupils and teachers, brothers and sisters, mums and dads, grannies and grandpas, animals and ghosts, in a range of styles and moods and of varying length. I asked a group of juniors to work in pairs, select one of the poems from the following selection and prepare it for performance in front of the class:

- 'You Can't Be That' by Brian Patten in *Thawing Frozen Frogs*, illustrated by David Mostyn, Viking.

- 'You Must be Jealous of Me' by Colin McNaughton in *Making Friends with Frankenstein: A Book of Monstrous Poems and Pictures*, Walker Books.

- 'Dialogue between My Cat Bridget and Me' in *Cat Among the Pigeons* by Kit Wright, illustrated by Posy Simmonds, Puffin.

- 'Excuses, Excuses' by Gareth Owen in *100 Best Poems for Children*, edited by Roger McGough and illustrated by Sheila Moxley, Puffin.

- 'Icarus' by Cynthia Rider and 'River Song' by Gerard Benson in *I've Got a Poem for You: Poems to Perform*, collected by John Foster and illustrated by Belle Mellor, Oxford University Press.

With a Year 5 class I looked at two anonymously written poems and then three of my own.

A CONVERSATION OVERHEARD

No school today?
Oh yes, school every day.
What did you do at school today?
Oh, we played games and sang and painted and danced,
We prayed and fought and laughed and cried.
Did you like school today?
No, nothing much happened.

91

'I,' SAID THE DONKEY

'I,' said the donkey, all shaggy and brown,
'Carried his mother, all into the town,
Carried her uphill, carried her down,
I,' said the donkey, all shaggy and brown.

'I,' said the cow, with spots of red,
'Gave him hay for to rest his head,
Gave him a manger for his bed.
I,' said the cow, with spots of red,

'I,' said the sheep, with twisted horn,
'Gave my wool for to keep him warm,
Gave my coat on Christmas morn.
I,' said the sheep, with twisted horn.

'I,' said the dove from the rafters high,
'Cooed him to sleep with a lullaby,
Cooed him to sleep, my mate and I.
I,' said the dove from the rafters high.

THE EXCUSE

No homework Simpkins?
No sir.
And what pray is the excuse this time?
Well sir …
No don't tell me, Simpkins, let me guess. The dog ate it?
No sir, we don't have a dog.
You sister was sick on it?
No sir, I'm an only child.
You left it on the bus?
No sir, I come to school on my bike.
Your father made the fire with it?
No sir, we have gas central heating.
Your granny threw it in the dustbin?
No sir, my granny's dead, sir.
A monster from outer space took it?
No sir, there are no such things as aliens.
A ghost spirited it away?
No sir, I don't believe in the supernatural.

Well, Simpkins, having exhausted all the possible reasons
  I can think of
for you not handing in your homework, I shall be most
  interested to know
what excuse you have?

Yes, sir.

Well?

You didn't set any homework this week, sir.

INTERROGATION IN THE NURSERY

Infant:	What's that?
INSPECTOR:	What?
Infant:	That on your face.
INSPECTOR:	It's a moustache
Infant:	What does it do?
INSPECTOR:	It doesn't do anything.
Infant:	Oh.
INSPECTOR:	It just sits there on my lip.
Infant:	Does it go up your nose?
INSPECTOR:	No.
Infant:	Could I stroke it?
INSPECTOR:	No.
Infant:	Is it alive?
INSPECTOR:	No.
Infant:	Can I have one?
INSPECTOR:	No.
Infant:	Why?
INSPECTOR:	Because little girls don't have moustaches.
Infant:	Why?
INSPECTOR:	Well, they just don't.
Infant:	Can I have one when I grow up?
INSPECTOR:	No.
Infant:	Why?
INSPECTOR:	Because ladies don't have moustaches either.
Infant:	Well, my grannie's got one!

(Published in *It Takes One to Know One*
by Gervase Phinn, Puffin)

93

BONFIRE NIGHT

'Dad, can I light a Sparkler?'

'No, no, and stay right back.'

'Dad, can I light a Catherine Wheel,
A Squib or Jumping Jack?
Dad, can I light a Banger,
A Rocket or Golden Rain,
Dad, can I light a Thunderflash?'

'Be quiet, you are a pain.
I've told you many times before,
Just leave it all to me,
Fireworks are dangerous, son.'

'But Dad—I'm 33!'

The children, working in pairs, then tried their hands at writing their own conversation poems. I gave them a number of guidelines.

Your conversation poem:

- might be in the form of a letter—to an auntie, the electricity board, a neighbour, pen-friend, the headteacher, a supermarket manager;

- could be a telephone poem to a doctor, dentist, teacher, relation, neighbour or friend;

- might be a conversation between:

  - mum or dad and a neighbour

  - two angry motorists

  - a policemen and a burglar

  - a king or queen and a beggar

  - a pupil and a teacher

  - two pupils

  - a mum or dad and a daughter or son

  - two animals

  - two ghosts

  - the wind and the sea

- needs to be rehearsed for performance—try out different voices.

Here is a conversation poem by David and Paul:

MOTHER AND SON

Mum: Don't stand on the doorstep come in.

Boy: I was just …

Mum: Hurry up there's a draught.

Boy: I know but …

Mum: Take your coat off.

Boy: Why?

Mum: Because I say so.

Boy: But …

Mum: And no buts.

Boy: You don't understand.

Mum: Your tea's nearly ready.

Boy: Listen a minute.

Mum: So go and wash your hands.

Boy: I can't.

Mum: Yes, you can.

Boy: I know I can wash my hands but …

Mum: Well, go and do it then.

Boy: But …

Mum: And then set the table.

Boy: Please will you listen?

Mum: And no television.

Boy: But …

Mum: And finish your homework before tea.

Boy: I finished my homework at school, but …

Mum: And put your slippers on.

Boy: Mrs Johnson!!!

Mum: Pardon?

Boy: Mrs Johnson, I've been trying to tell you.

Mum: What?

Boy: I'm not your son and you're not my mum.

Mum: I'm not your mum and you're not my son?

Boy: No. I live next door.

Chapter 16
Poems from Other Cultures

Some of the poems sing, and you can read them as though you were listening to a catchy tune. Others speak to you and urge you to think, to meditate on an atmosphere or a feeling.

Farrukh Dhondy, *Ranters, Ravers and Rhymers: Poems by Black and Asian Poets*, Lions

---

Poetry encompasses all religions and cultures and children should be exposed to the richness of verse forms from other countries and which reflect the varied experiences and cultural diversity of the people with whom we share the planet. By reading, discussing and studying poetry from other cultures we can help break down the barriers between cultures and encourage respect and understanding.

There is splendid verve and energy about much Black and Asian poetry. Chinese and Japanese poetry have a simplicity and freshness which appeals to children and which can act as models for their own writing.

There is a wide variety of different forms of poetry from other cultures ranging from magic incantations to nonsense poems, lullabies to love songs, reggae lyrics to calypso. Many of the poems contained in the selection below explore such topics as growing up, family, place, the seasons, relationships, customs, festivals and food, and are particularly vivid and rhythmic and ideal for reading aloud and performing.

- *Wicked World!* by Benjamin Zephaniah, Puffin.

- *The Oxford Book of Children's Poetry* edited by Michael Harrison and Christopher Stuart-Clark, Oxford University Press.

- *Talking Turkeys* by Benjamin Zephaniah, Viking.

- *Come on into My Tropical Garden* by Grace Nichols, Curtis Brown.

- *I Din Do Nuttin'* by John Agard, Bodley Head.

- *Poetry Jump Up: A Collection of Black Poetry,* compiled by Grace Nichols and illustrated by Michael Lewis, Puffin.

- *Playing a Dazzler* by James Berry, Hamish Hamilton.

- *Mangoes and Bullets: Selected and New Poems 1972–84* by John Agard, Pluto Press.

- *The Penguin Book of Chinese Verse,* translated by Robert Kotewall and Norman L. Smith, and edited by A. R. Davis, Penguin.

- *The Puffin Book of Utterly Brilliant Poetry*, edited by Brian Patten, Puffin.

Chapter 17
Poems from Experience

A poem is not an object, fixed in space and time with a single, unmoveable meaning. It is a living organism which we can study, match with our own experience of life, and of which we may make something new every day.

Charles Causley, *The Puffin Book of Magic Verse*, Puffin

Stories and anecdotes which draw on children's experiences can be the basis for poetry which is honest and evocative. The teacher might encourage children to recall a memorable event or re-tell an interesting experience and then sharpen that observation and help with the initial ideas and early drafts.

With an older junior class we discussed two of my more thoughtful poems.

CHRISTMAS EVE

Christmas lights twinkled in the shopping arcade
That Christmas Eve.
Giant plastic Santas smiled
And mud-brown reindeers pranced across the walls.
Tinny voices of taped carol singers filled the air.
People rushed and pushed,
Hurried and scurried,
To buy the last of the presents.

And on the bench before the crib
Sat an old woman in shabby coat
And shapeless woollen hat,
Clutching an empty threadbare bag,
And smiling at the Baby Jesus.

(Published in *A Wayne in a Manger*
by Gervase Phinn, Penguin)

WHEN I WAS A BOY

When I was a boy:
My bunk bed was a pirate ship
That sailed the seven seas,
My sheets they were the silvery sails
That fluttered in the breeze.

I'd dream of clashing cutlasses
And the crack, crack, crack of the gun,
And the boom, boom, boom of the cannons
And the heat of the tropical sun.

I'd dream of far-off oceans
And treasure by the ton,
And mountainous waves
And watery graves
And islands in the sun.

Collections which conjure up the brightest and clearest pictures of family life, school and the world around us are:

- *100 Best Poems for Children*, edited by Roger McGough and illustrated by Sheila Moxley, Puffin.

- *The Puffin Book of Fantastic First Poems*, edited by June Crebbin, Puffin.

- *The Tortoise had a Mighty Roar* by Peter Dixon, Macmillan.

- *Ghostly Riders* by Phil Carradice, Pont.

- *Funny Poems to Give You the Giggles*, collected by Susie Gibbs, Oxford University Press.

- *The Hat* by Carol Ann Duffy, Faber & Faber.

- *Wicked World!* by Benjamin Zephaniah, Puffin.

- *Mustard, Custard, Grumble Belly and Gravy* by Michael Rosen, illustrated by Quentin Blake, Bloomsbury Children's Books.

- *Cat Among the Pigeons* by Kit Wright, illustrated by Posy Simmonds, Puffin.

- *Thawing Frozen Frogs* by Brian Patten, Viking.

In the following four poems by junior-age children the language has a freshness and vigour as the young writers recreate their memories with skill and imagination.

FACE AT THE WINDOW

Mrs Harvey lived across the road.
She was a tall woman with a cracked creased skin like an
   old leather handbag,
Bright peering eyes and small unsmiling little mouth.
She watched from her front room—a pale face at the
   window.
On my way to school I avoided her stare.
When the snow came an ambulance took her away.
I never saw Mrs Harvey again.

(Jayne)

CASUALTY

The hospital was too warm and smelt of disinfectant.
The chairs were too hard and the lights too bright.
The walls were a sickly cream and the windows long and
   high.

Everyone stared at one another.
Everyone looked scared and uncomfortable.
Everyone wished they were somewhere else.

I waited quietly with my mum until my name was called,
And held her hand when the doctor came,
And cried in the car on the way home.

(Thomas)

LOST AND FOUND

On the camp site my little sister got lost.
She wandered off by herself.
Mum and Dad shouted and shouted at me,
'Why didn't you look after her?'
Later, we found her asleep in the tent.

(Paul)

SCHOOL TRIP

On our school trip we went to London.
We saw skyscrapers and palaces,
Museums and parks,
Congested roads and crowded stations,
Rushing people and marching soldiers,
But I remember most
The man in the cardboard box
Holding out an empty bean tin
And begging for money.

(Rebecca)

Chapter 18
Poems from the Environment

The most important thing to say about a poem is that it doesn't need to be a poem. Write what you want to write and make it a poem later.

George Macbeth

Exploring the environment is a good means of offering stimuli for poetry writing and frequently generates some really impressive poetry. The choice of location depends a great deal on the time available and access to the places you wish to visit. It could be a short excursion outside within the school's grounds or a day trip to the sea, a castle, a river or a museum.

Preparation is important and prior to exploring the environment there needs to be a briefing. All children will be equipped with a notebook and a pencil and told to jot down words, phrases, ideas, images—anything that interests them when they are outside. They are told that when they arrive at the location to have a good look around them and choose those things which interest them and might be the subject of a poem to be written up later in class. It might be something small such as an insect or a leaf, something large like a gnarled old oak tree or a building. They are asked to jot down all the things that come to mind when they observe their chosen subject—size, shape, colour, texture—and try to invent some similes. The teacher might do the exercise the pupils have been set or discuss with individual children his or her topic and approach, offering ideas and suggestions for improvement.

On returning to the classroom the teacher will ask the children to discuss what they have seen and written and to study the notes which might be turned into a poem. Which parts do we keep? Which parts do we discard? Which parts might we develop? The poem might be short or long, a description or an expression of feeling, rhyming or non-rhyming.

A Year 6 class visited a local church. They spent some time walking around the dark and atmospheric interior before exploring the graveyard and examining the various headstones. They were asked to note down their observations, what they saw, touched, smelt, heard, read on the tablets on the walls and carved on the tombstones and what they felt. Here are three of their poems based on the visit.

IN THE CHURCHYARD

On the smooth rounded marble slab,
Poking though the weedy grass
Like a giant's wet grey tongue,
Are faded curving letters
Glistening in the cold November rain.
'Here lyeth Mary Bower Broomhead
Beloved wife of Francis Bower Broomhead.
She is not dead but sleepeth in the arms of God.'

THE STAINED GLASS SOLDIER

How proud he stands,
The soldier in the stained glass window,
Shining armour,
Sword held high in his hand,
Shield with cross of silver,
Helmet with the fancy feather,
A golden halo around his head.
How proud he looks,
The soldier in the stained glass window,
Up there above the altar,
Lit by the sunlight,
Staring down,
On us
Below.

CHURCH MOUSE

A mouse lives here,
Behind the little hole,
Beneath the old wooden pulpit,
Waiting in the dusty darkness
For night when all is still.
Then he will scamper along the floor,
And scratch along the pews,
And scurry to the porch,
To nibble at the hymnbooks.

A Year 5 and 6 group visited the Yorkshire coast where the teacher encouraged the children to look, listen, touch and smell. They walked from Sandsend to Whitby, collecting pebbles, shells, smooth sea glass and bits of jet, and once in the town they climbed the 199 steps to the Abbey before visiting the Captain Cook Museum and the Grand Turk sailing ship moored in the quay.

Here are a selection of the jottings of three pupils, Jacob, Jamuna and Maya, before they structured them into poems later when they returned to school:

Gannets swooping, cormorants diving, children
splashing.
rocks like broken teeth, rattling pebbles, high black cliffs,
curving waves, cold grey empty sky, muddy mounds,
plastic bottle bent, rubber sole of a shoe, rotting fish,
smooth wood washed on the waves.

(Jacob)

Grey oily sea, screeching seagulls,
soft white sand, worn stone steps,
rigging like a spider's web,
deck shiny with polish and water.

(Jamuna)

Smell of fish and chips and candyfloss and seaweed
rotting in the sun, sand rippled by the sea, swooping
seagulls, shells like toenails, bits of polished glass,
green and white, seaweed purple and brown and crunchy
under your feet, bobbing boats, pale pebbles and jagged
rocks.

(Maya)

Chapter 19
Poems from Poems

Poetry is like an all devouring monster. It devours scraps of language from whenever and wherever it can: clichés, sports commentaries, letters, political speeches, science reports, newscasts, proverbs, shopping lists, other poems—any rhetorical device or linguistic structure can be and is used by poets.

Michael Rosen, *I See a Voice*, Thames

Children can be helped in the shaping of their own experiences by reading the poetry of others. When they read poems by Brian Patten, Wendy Cope, Ogden Nash, Irene Rawnsley, Judith Nicholls, Seamus Heaney, Edward Lear, Grace Nichols, James Reeves, J. R. R. Tolkien, John Kitching, Joan Aiken, Charles Causley, Peter Dixon, Elizabeth Jennings, Sylvia Plath, Michael Rosen, Wes Magee and many more fine poets, they are often reminded of experiences they themselves have had and given possible structures for shaping those memories. Over the year the teacher might heighten the children's awareness by reading a wide range of poems: poems that surprise and please, that make them think, laugh, feel sad; poems with strong rhythms, solemn lyrics, limericks, ballads, concrete verse, shape poems, acrostics, chants and charms, Caribbean verse, poems from Africa, Asia and from around Europe.

In the following poems, written by Year 6 pupils, Dominic, Joanne, Jessica and David, the young poets imitate the styles and structures of popular published writers.

UPS AND DOWNS

Parents like you
to:
tidy your room,
make your bed,
do your homework,
and come in early.

Parents like you
to:
brush your teeth,
comb your hair,
wash behind your ears,
and clean your shoes.

Parents like you
to:
eat your cabbage,
sit up properly,

wash the dishes,
and turn the television off.

Parents like you
to:
be quiet,
be sensible,
be polite,
and speak nicely.

Parents like you
to:
behave as they think they did when they were our age.

(Based on 'Ups and Downs' by June Crebbin in
The Crocodile is Coming!, Walker Books)

MY IMAGINARY BOX

I will put in my box:

thick toast with a layer of melting butter,
crispy chips, hot and fat,
cold, dark chocolate ice cream.

I will put in my box:

the sound of the sea on the sandy shore,
the pop of the seaweed ,
the crunch of the pebbles under my feet.

I will put in my box:

Dad's cheering when I score a goal,
Mum's singing when she's making tea,
Grannie's snoring when she's fast asleep.

I will put in my box:

the smell of pine trees,
Christmas lights and coloured wrapping paper,
a carpet of snow on the lawn outside.

My box will be made of shining silver
And smell of soap and flowers.
It will have secret drawers and a heavy lock
And I will keep the key.

(Based on 'The Magic Box' by Kit Wright first published in *Cat Among the Pigeons*,
by Kit Wright, illustrated by Posy Simmons, Puffin, 1987)

IN A CLASS OF HIS OWN

Barry is best at everything in our class!
His reading is clearer,
His writing is neater,
His spelling is better,
His speaking is nicer!

Barry is best at everything in our class!
His running is quicker,
His jumping is higher,
His swimming is faster
His singing is louder!

Barry is best at everything in our class!
His teeth are whiter,
His hands are cleaner,
His shoes are brighter,
His clothes are smarter!

In our class Barry is the best.
And his head is much, much bigger than the rest!

(Based on 'Barry' by Mick Gowar in
Third Time Lucky, Viking Kestrel)

SCHOOL TRIP

On our school trip …
Jane Tomlinson stayed too long in the sun,
And burnt her arms, legs and face,
And had to stay in the hospital.

On our school trip …
William Ellis dropped his purse down a grate,
And tried to get it back and got his fingers caught,
And cried for the rest of the day.

On our school trip …
Mr Johnson slipped on a rock and fell in the sea.
Miss Draper tried to grab him and fell in too,
And her bag disappeared in the slimy weeds.

On our school trip …
Wayne was sick on Jennifer, who was sick on Jason,
Who was sick on Wayne.
Wayne was sick again.

On our school trip …
The bus driver hit a car and his wing mirror fell off.
He shouted and shouted and blamed the teachers
For not making us sit down.

On our school trip …
Becky got lost in the amusements and a policeman
    brought her back
And said Miss Draper ought to be more careful
Letting children go off by themselves.

I don't think I'll go on the school trip next year.
It was really, really boring!

(Based on 'School Trip' by Gervase Phinn in
It Takes One to Know One, Puffin)

WHAT A WEEK!

On Monday I missed my breakfast
Because of oversleeping.

On Tuesday I got stomach ache
Because of overeating.

On Wednesday I grazed my knee
Because I tripped and fell.

On Thursday I was late for class
Because I didn't hear the bell.

On Friday I dropped my coat
Running out of school.

On Saturday I went swimming
And was pushed into the pool.

On Sunday I stayed in bed
Sleeping, dreaming, snoring.

After the week that I've just had—
I found it rather boring!

('What a Week' is adapted from the original poem 'I Only Asked' by Gervase Phinn
first published in *It's My Dog*, compiled by John Foster, Oxford University Press, 1994)

Chapter 20
Poems from Photographs and Paintings

The essential quality of poetry is that it makes a new effort of attention and discovers a new world within a known world.

D. H. Lawrence, *Introductions and Reviews* edited by N. H. Reeve and John Worthen,

---

Looking at a photograph can trigger ideas, impressions and feelings which can be stimuli for writing poetry. Over the years I have built up a large and varied collection of photographs of people, places, scenes and buildings, some taken by my son, Matthew, and some others from the National Portrait Gallery.

Working with Year 5 and 6 talented children on a Creative Writing Day, I asked each of them to study the photograph before them on the desk. Each pupil was given a different view of a building. The photographs included stately homes, back-to-back terraces, thatched cottages, moated castles, Regency crescents and high-rise flats. They were then asked a series of questions:

Who lives here?

What is the owner's name?

What is the exterior of the building like?

Walk through the front door. What you see?

What does the building smell of?

What can you hear inside?

Go into the first room. What is on the floor, walls, shelves and ceiling?

Climb the stairs. What do you see?

Peter's photograph depicted a large four-storey dilapidated terraced house with railings at the front, broken guttering and an impressively large front door. There was a 'To Let' sign outside. In our discussion about the focus of his poem he commented that no one would want to live in such a run-down house. I suggested he imagine he was looking for a place to rent and was being shown around by the landlord. After two drafts he was then given some help in structuring his poem. It takes the form of a monologue.

THE HOUSE FOR RENT

Do come in.
You do not need to wipe your feet.
The carpet's old and worn and needs replacing anyway.
Ignore the smell.
The house has been empty for so long.
I think it must be damp or cats or the dustbins out the
back.
It's very dark in here, I know,
But when the walls are painted it will be brighter
And will cover up the stains.
The ceiling does have cracks, but those will be repaired,
And don't worry about the broken glass.
I'll sweep it up after you've gone.
Do take care upon the stairs.
They are rather wobbly, I'm afraid.
The banister's come loose
And there are missing floorboards.
That door on the landing doesn't open.
The handle came off in my hand.
The bathroom's very large.
The shower doesn't work but will be fixed.
Don't worry about the leaking pipe
And the toilet that won't flush.
I'll get a plumber to come round.
The broken tiles will also be replaced
And the light will soon be working.
Those mice get everywhere.
I'll put some traps down.
You will get used to the noise and the shuddering.
It's quite handy having the station so close.
Well, now that you've looked around
Do you think you might like to live here?

I said earlier that poets, like artists, look carefully at their subjects, then select the very best words to describe them. Paintings of faces and figures provide excellent stimuli for poetry writing. Children might be encouraged to study a painting, carefully concentrating on the shapes, colours, distinctive features, dress, facial expressions and surroundings. *Give Me Your Hand* is a superb collection of poetry by the brilliant Irish writer Paul Durcan inspired by the paintings in the National Gallery in London. On each page is a poem alongside a painting by Rubens, Leonardo, Rembrandt, Watteau, Goya, Michelangelo, Puget, Degas, Velázquez, Gainsborough, Reynolds and many more. This gave me the idea to present a group of Year 6 pupils with a selection of reproduction pictures and portraits (some purchased from Mainstone Publications, Sparham, Norwich, Norfolk NR9 5AQ and others from the National Portrait Gallery, St Martin's Place, London WC2H OHE) as an inspiration for their verse. The children were asked a series of questions about each painting:

Who is this person?

What is his or her name?

How old is he or she?

Where does he or she live?

What colour are the eyes, hair, skin?

How would you describe the expression (scowling, grimacing, sheepish, deadpan, angry, gentle, guilty-looking)?

What is the person feeling (happy, depressed, angry, envious, bitter)?

What is the person looking at?

What sounds can he or she hear?

Where does the person live?

Prior to looking at their own painting for study the children were given a postcard size reproduction of the painting by Charles Spencelayh (1865–1958) entitled *Why War?*, which is displayed in the Harris Museum and Art Gallery in Preston. The postcards were purchased at the gallery shop.

The painting depicts an elderly war veteran sitting in a Windsor chair, his hands clasped in front of him. He is looking sad and thoughtful. There is a newspaper on another chair, the front page of which shows a picture of Neville Chamberlain and the headline 'Premier Flying to Hitler'. It is a massively detailed painting and the children soon volunteered an amazing range of ideas. They were not aware of the title at first but I directed their attention to some of the objects in the painting—the strip of medal ribbons on the man's coat, the gas mask on the table, the small marble bust of Napoleon on the shelf, the painting of the death of Nelson on the wall, the soldier's helmet and the violin. They soon guessed that the subject of the painting is a war veteran who probably leads a lonely life in his untidy and cluttered sitting room. We discussed the First World War in which the man had taken part and the children were given some information. I then asked the children to give the man a name and a voice and to write a monologue in his voice: What is going through his mind, his memories, his feelings now and his thoughts for the future? In a relatively short time the range of responses helped to build up a strong impression of the person featured in the picture. They were asked to put themselves in the man's shoes. I particularly like Mark's poem. I suggested he repeat some lines to get a more powerful effect.

ANOTHER WAR

We were told that it was the last war,
The war to end all wars.
We were told it would never happen again,
All that mud, all that killing.
We were told that things would get better,
That we would never have to fight again,
That no one in the future would have to die,
That bombs would never fall again,
And buildings would stay standing.
That's what we were told.
That's what we were told.

Each pupil was then given a different print and asked to write a short poem based upon it. They could describe the character, imagine what he or she was thinking, write a monologue or a conversation poem or tell a story in verse about the person. The range of poetry produced was wide and impressive:

A father—hunched, his arms tightly folded across
his chest.
A mother—bent in sorrow, her arms hidden in the
old shawl.
Both barefoot, both with dead eyes looking down.
A boy—feels with his fingers, touching them.
His eyes wide and blue.

(*The Tragedy* by Pablo Picasso,
National Gallery of Art, Washington DC)

He has a big wide, friendly face,
A merry morning face,
Hidden in a tangle of curls.
Green eyes peer through
Lips and cheeks as red as his postbox.

(*Portrait of Joseph Roulin by* Vincent van Goph,
Museum of Modern Art, New York,)

Oil on canvas, 25 3/8 x 21 3/4' (64.6 x 55.2 cm). Gift of Mr. and Mrs. William A. M. Burden, Mr. and Mrs. Raul Rosenberg, Nelson A. Rockefeller, Mr. and Mrs. Armand Bartos, Sidney and Harriet Janis, Mr. and Mrs. Werner E. Josten, and Loula D. Lasker Bequest (by exchange). 196.1989. © 2008. Digital image, The Museum of Modern Art, New York/Scala, Florence

A tall grim figure in black.
His fingers are like twigs.
Great bushy beard,
And deep dark eyes.

(*Self Portrait* by Henri Rousseau, Narodni Gallery, Prague)

You're in real trouble!
All innocent as if it wasn't your fault.
When your father gets home you'll be for it.
He told you not to wear his hat.
Now look at it!
Torn and tattered with the brim hanging off.
You're in real trouble you are!

(*The Torn Hat* by Thomas Sully,
Museum of Fine Arts, Boston)

It looks as if her head's on fire,
Great flaming hat as red as a furnace,
Burning the golden hair.

(*Child with Red Hat* by Mary Cassatt,
Clark Art Institute, Massachusetts)

This is a dreamy face,
A faraway look is in her eyes.
She thinks of the adventures in the story.
Her golden hair falls like a mane
Tickling her shoulders.
She tightly clutches her book
And wishes she were inside the covers.

(*The Story Book* by William Adolphe Bouguereau,
Los Angeles County Museum of Art)

Why are you staring at me? says the face.
Get on with what you are doing
And leave me to stare at the view.
She does not smile and her blue eyes look cold.
Although her cheeks are red and her face is round
and pink,
She is ill.
Sitting all straight and covered in thick clothes,
Wrapped up in a blanket on such a sunny day.
She is out of place at the seaside.

(*By the Seashore* by Pierre-Auguste Renoir,
Metropolitan Museum of Art, New York)

She yawns with a mouth like a gaping cave
In a face as fat as a football.
She has the fists of a boxer
And arms as thick as tree trunks.
It's all that ironing.

(*The Ironers* by Edgar Degas, Musée du Louvre, Paris)

The little boy plays but no one listens.
He puffs out his cheeks and blows.
His fingers, like little sausages, hold the flute tightly.
He plays with all his might,
But no one's in the mood for music.
No one listens—not even the dog.

(*Peasant Family in an Interior* by Louis Le Nain,
Musée du Louvre, Paris)

Other paintings which stimulated a range of imaginative responses were:

- *Mrs Mounter* by Harold Gilman, Walker Art Gallery, Liverpool.

- *Two Jamaican Girls* by Augustus John, Walker Art Gallery, Liverpool.

- *The Small Cowper Madonna* by Raphael, National Gallery of Art, Washington DC.

- *Domino Players* by Horace Pippin, Phillips Collection, Washington DC.

- *The Oyster Gatherers at Cancale* by John Singer Sargent, Corcoran Gallery of Art, Washington DC.

- *The Gypsy Woman with Baby* by Amedeo Modigliani, National Gallery of Art, Washington DC.

- *The Milkmaid* by Johannes Vermeer, The Rijksmuseum, Amsterdam.

- *The Letter* by Johannes Vermeer, The Rijksmuseum, Amsterdam.

- *Christina's World* by Andrew Wyeth, Museum of Modern Art, New York.

- *In the Studio* by William Merritt Chase, Brooklyn Museum, New York.

- *Susan Comforting the Baby* by Mary Cassatt, Museum of Fine Arts, Houston.

Chapter 21

A Poetry Project: Myths and Legends

> Myth is how we explain the enigma to ourselves, in private and as a tribe: there is a sun god, a god of love; colours mean jealousy, rage, peace; abstract ideas and emotions become birds, trees, legendary beasts.
>
> Gillian Clarke, *Myth, Life, The Universe and Everything*
> in the Poetry Resources File of the Poetry Society

Myths, legends and folktales provide rich material for poetry and give children the chance to use their imaginations to the full. I visited a primary school over the course of a term to work with a Year 6 group. As part of their topic on the Egyptians, and later on the Romans and the Vikings, we had talked, read and written about some of the myths and legends associated with these fascinating peoples. From here developed a poetry project: Myths and Legends from Around the World.

Initial ideas

In groups of four the children were asked to jot down very brief details of as many myths, legends and folk tales they could think of and the names of any fabulous creatures or mythical monsters they could remember. These were later typed into a list for future reference and research.

Initial reading

Some short factual prose accounts were read and discussed. 'The Legend of the Lambton Worm' which follows was typical:

> The son of the Lord of the Manor, Lord Lambton was fishing in the River Wear near the great stone-towered Lambton Castle in Northumberland. He caught a strange eel-like fish and on his way home threw it into the well at the Castle and thought no more about it. Many years later when the son of Lord Lambton was away fighting in the Crusades the worm wriggled out of the well. It was now huge and black and began to terrify the neighbourhood eating sheep, cattle and any living thing it could catch.

> At night it slept coiled nine times around a great hill. All attempts to kill it failed. If it was cut in two the halves merely joined back together again. When the son returned from the Crusades he was told by a local witch to cover his armour with sharp spikes and fight the monster in the river. For her help the witch demanded that the son should kill the first living thing to greet him from the castle after his victory. The son agreed expecting his father to release a dog as had been planned. The witch's advice worked. As the worm coiled itself around the son it was cut into many pieces which were carried away in the river before they could rejoin themselves. Returning to the castle after his victory the son expected to see the dog running to greet him but in his excitement his father had forgotten and came out himself to greet his son. Naturally the son refused to kill the old man. The witch

in her fury put a curse on the family that no male Lambton would die peacefully in his bed.

This factual account was compared with the poem I wrote:

THE LEGEND OF THE LAMBTON WORM

There's a very famous story
About a serpent and a well,
The story of the Lambton Worm,
A story I will tell.

It happened one fine Monday
In the forest near a lake,
That the Lord of Lambton Castle
Came upon a snake.

It was a tiny wriggly thing
With a rather fishy smell,
So the Lord of Lambton Castle
Dropped it down a nearby well.

Then he forgot about it
And went fighting far away,
But the worm it grew and grew
To be slimy, fat and grey.

One day it slithered from the well
And roaring like a leopard,
It swallowed up a flock of sheep,
The sheepdog and the shepherd.

For years and years the creature lived
Devouring all it saw,
When one day brave Lord Lambton
Came back from the war.

He put his helmet on his head
And with his sword and shield,
He climbed up every mountain and
He looked in every field.

Until he found the Lambton Worm
With eyes of fiery red,
And he lifted up his great sharp sword
And chopped off the big black head.

Then he cut it into pieces
And he dropped it down the well
And that was the end of the Lambton Worm,
So story-tellers tell.

(Published in *Family Phantoms* by Gervase Phinn, Puffin)

A number of other poems and prose extracts were then read including:

- 'The Coming of Grendel' from *Beowulf*, translated by Gerard Benson in *Poems on the Underground*, compiled by Gerard Benson, Judith Clark and Cicely Herbert, Orion.

- 'The Last Dragon' by Ian Larmont in *Dragon Poems* edited by John Foster and Korky Paul, Oxford University Press.

- Extract from 'The Kraken' by Alfred Lord Tennyson.

- 'Jabberwocky' by Lewis Carroll in *100 Best Poems for Children*, edited by Roger McGough and illustrated by Sheila Moxley, Puffin.

- 'Amparo's Journey' in *The Golden Turtle and Other Tales* by Gervase Phinn, Collins.

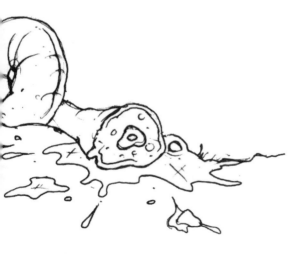

The process of drafting

I read two of my own poems, 'The Nokk' and 'Leviathan', and talked about the process of creative writing—the initial ideas, the research I carried out, the drafting, rewriting and editing.

THE NOKK

Be warned you little children
Every son and every daughter
Who disobey your mums and dads
And go too close to water.

For in every river, stream and brook,
In lake and pond and loch,
In waterfalls steep and chasms deep,
There lurks the deadly Nokk.

His beard is of a weedy green,
His ears like giant oars,
His eyes are the hue of the ocean blue,
And his hands are giant claws.

He sits and waits in his watery cave,
And never makes a noise,
Or silently swims near the surface clear
Looking for girls and boys.

And should he spy a child like you,
Playing near waters deep,
With his click-clack jaws and his snip-snap claws
He'll grab you by the feet.

Then he'll drag you down to the murky depths,
To the watery world of the fish,
And on his rock, the deadly Nokk,
Will eat his tasty dish.

So be warned you little children,
And obey your parents do.
Every son and every daughter, stay away from the water,
Or his next meal could be you!

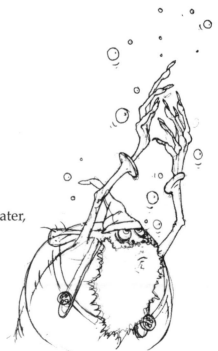

LEVIATHAN

There are salt sea tales
Of great white whales
And monsters of the Deep,
Of the red-eyed shark
Which swims in the dark
And never ever sleeps.
There are octopuses
The size of buses,
And a clam with an iron jaw,
Gargantuan rays,
Which spend their days
On the ocean's sandy floor.

There are mariners' yarns
Of fish with arms
And squids that can squeeze you to death.
Of mermaids fair
With seaweed hair
That can turn you to stone with their breath.
There are fire-breathing eels
And two-headed seals
And a crab with a giant claw,
Pale creatures of jelly
That lay on their belly,
On the ocean's sandy floor.

But such legends of old
Don't compare with those told
Of the greatest sea monster of all.
Its long deadly tail
Is covered in scales
And its head is a fiery ball.
The teeth sharp and white
Have a venomous bite
And it utters a deafening roar.
The huge eyes they glow
As it drags you below
To the ocean's sandy floor.

(Published in *Family Phantoms* by Gervase Phinn, Puffin)

Providing reference and research material

The School Library Service put together a comprehensive Book Box based on the theme and included stories, poems, booklets, visitors' guides and specialist reference material. The collection included:

- *The Book of Dragons* by J. Allen and J. Griffiths, Orbis Publishers.

- *A Dictionary of British Folk Tales* by K. Briggs, Taylor & Francis.

- *Mythical Monsters* by C. Gould, W. H. Allen.

- *A Dictionary of Fabulous Beasts* by R. Barber and A. Riches, Boydell Press.

- *Curious Myths of the Middle Ages* by the Rev. S. Baring-Gould, Boydell Press.

- *The Book of Imaginary Beings* by J. L. Borges and M. Guerrero, Jonathan Cape.

- *Readers Digest Illustrated Reverse Dictionary.*

Writing the poems

The pupils were encouraged to undertake some research about their chosen myth, legend or fabulous creature. They jotted down words, phrases and ideas. I looked through the notes they had gathered and suggested some openings and structures they might like to try. Some wrote free verse poems, others were keen to compose rhyming couplets, two wrote acrostics and several more tried their hands at concrete verse. I asked the pupils to focus carefully on their choice of words, rearrange the word sequence and compare the effect, change a comparison into a metaphor to see if the image worked better, alter word order in a line to make the rhythm work, and use alliteration, repetition and onomatopoeic words to add to the vividness of the poem. This process of expanding and condensing their work is necessary; most poets go through it. The National Curriculum demands that later in their school careers pupils should be given such opportunities to extend and refine their competence in drafting and redrafting, and such groundwork in primary school can be valuable and productive.

Display and anthology

At the conclusion of the project a large colourful display of poetry, pictures and illuminated writing was mounted and the children's efforts were collected into a small booklet of verse. 'The Phoenix' by Cara and 'The Night Visitor' by Max give a flavour of the content:

THE PHOENIX

You can see him in the firelight
In the flickering flames,
Wings of yellow and red
Fluttering in the heat,
A curved beak as black as coal,
Eyes like embers and
claws as hot as a furnace.
When the phoenix is burnt to ashes
He is born again.

THE NIGHT VISITOR

He waits for midnight
And when the moon shines in a black sky,
He climbs from his dark and dusty coffin,
And flutters in the air like a bat.
His eyes are blood red and his hands are claws,
His face as white as chalk.
He's searching for his prey tonight.
The vampire's on the loose.
So lock your windows, bolt your doors,
Or his next victim might be YOU!

Chapter 22
Poems of Praise

Good poetry does undoubtedly tend to form the soul and character; it tends to beget a love of beauty and truth in alliance together; it suggests, however indirectly, high and noble principles of action, it inspires the emotion so helpful in making principles operative. Hence its extreme importance to all of us.

Matthew Arnold, *Reports on Elementary Schools 1852–1882*
edited by Sir Francis Sandford

Children of all ages are able to write prayers and poems of praise. They hear passages from the Old and New Testaments of the Bible, extracts from the Koran, the Rig Veda, the Bhagavad Gita, the Sri Guru Granth Sahib and other sacred texts at assembly time and sing hymns of praise and thanksgiving. I worked with a group of ten and eleven year olds in a small Roman Catholic primary school and we composed our own prayers and poems of praise. We looked in some detail at a small selection of the more familiar modern and older prayers including 'St Patrick's Breastplate', 'Prayer of St Francis' and the 'Lord's Prayer' and we discussed the poetic devices such as repetition and contrast which are often featured. We also read and discussed the following prayers:

God be in my head, and in my understanding;
God be in mine eyes, and in my looking;
God be in my mouth, and in my speaking;
God be in my heart, and in my thinking;
God be at mine end, and at my parting.

Book of Hours (1514)

Teach us, good Lord, to serve you as you deserve;
to give and not to count the cost;
to fight and not to heed the wounds;
to toil, and not to seek for rest;
to labour and to ask for no reward;
save that of knowing that we do your will;
through Jesus Christ our Lord.

'Prayer of St Ignatius'

One unfamiliar prayer we particularly liked was written by William Barclay, a part of which follows:

O God, our Father, help us through this day to be:
>Cheerful when things go wrong;
>Persevering when things are difficult;
>Serene when things are irritating.

Enable us to be: Helpful to those in difficulties;
>Kind to those in need;
>Sympathetic to those whose hearts are sore;

Grant that: Nothing may make us lose our tempers
>Nothing may take away our joy
>Nothing may ruffle our peace;
>Nothing may make us bitter towards anyone.

A selection of prayers, psalms and poems of praise were made available and the children were encouraged to browse and read before writing a prayer of their own. This selection included:

- To every thing there is a season, Ecclesiastes 3: i–viii.

- St Paul's Epistle to the Corinthians, 1 Corinthians.

- The Song of Solomon.

- 'Benediction' by James Berry in *Poems on the Underground*, compiled by Gerard Benson, Judith Chernaik and Cicely Herbert, Orion.

- 'St Francis and the Birds' by Seamus Heaney from *Death of a Naturalist*, Faber & Faber.

- 'For the Christening of the Princess Elizabeth, Later to be Queen Elizabeth the First', William Shakespeare.

- 'Pied Beauty' by Gerard Manley Hopkins from *The Poems of Gerard Manley Hopkins*, Oxford University Press.

We compiled a small anthology of prayers written by the children, some of which were read in assembly over the year. Here is a sample:

When I feel sad help me to remember the happy times.
When I am scared help me to be brave.
When I get angry calm me down.
And when I am mean remind me of all things I've got.

>(Philip)

Bless all those who help others.
Those who:
> Care for the homeless,
> Feed the hungry,
> Look after the old people,
> Teach the young people,
> Nurse the sick,
> Listen to the lonely.

(Donna)

Thank you for all the bright things in the world—
> The sunshine, the flowers, the sparkling waters.
Thank you for all the dark things in the world—
> The deep mysterious caves, the black night.
Thank you for the big things in the world—
> Elephants and skyscrapers, mountains and whales.
Thank you for the little things in the world—
> Tiny shrews and insects and grains of sand.
Thank you for the fast things and the slow things,
> For the sweet things and the sour,
And help us to look after them.

(Rachel)

Chapter 23
Poets in School

THE PROPER POET

Today we have a real-live poet in school—
This gentleman who's standing next to me.
I must say when I met him in the entrance,
He was not as I imagined he would be.

I'd always thought that poets were tall and wan,
With eyes as dark and deep as any sea,
So when I saw this jolly little man,
He didn't seem a proper poet to me.

The poets I've seen in pictures dress in black
With velvet britches buttoned at the knee,
So when I saw the T-shirt and the jeans,
He didn't look a proper poet to me.

I've read that famous poets are often ill,
And die consumptive deaths on a settee.
Well, I've never seen a healthier-looking man,
He just didn't seem a proper poet to me.

My favourite poems are by Tennyson and Keats,
This modern stuff is not my cup of tea,
So when I heard our poet was keen on rap,
He didn't seem a proper poet to me.

Well, I'm certain that we'll all enjoy his poems
And listen—after all we've paid his fee—
I hope that they're in verses and they rhyme,
For that is proper poetry to me.

(Published in *The Day Our Teacher Went Batty*
by Gervase Phinn, Puffin)

The visit of a professional poet increases children's enjoyment of poetry and teaches them so much about technique. Poets like Peter Dixon, Levi Tafari, Ian McMillan, Graham Mort, Berlie Doherty and June Crebbin lift the printed word off the page and perform their poems with all the nuances of pace, timing and intonation. They talk to the children about their inspiration, why they choose particular words and phrases and the difficulties they experience in writing their poems. They suggest well-tried approaches and techniques and demonstrate that poetry is not some esoteric or precious activity and that adults as well as children write poetry too.

Who do I invite?

The Poetry Society, regional arts boards and the local English adviser and literacy consultant can recommend poets used to working with children and can supply references from headteachers in schools where the poets have worked. Colleagues in other schools in which poets have been well received generated enthusiasm in the children for poetry and run successful workshops, which are also valuable sources of information. Publishers will be happy to pass on letters to their poets and their addresses can be found at the front of their books.

Preparing for the visit

Preparation is vital. It is essential to plan the visit carefully and to budget for a planning meeting with the poet on extended schemes. Discussion with the poet is needed prior to the visit and basic considerations like the fee, travel arrangements and the programme for the day firmed up. If possible the initial approach should be made by letter, detailing suggested dates and times and outlining some general ideas about what the teacher hopes the visit will involve. The first enquiry can then be followed up by telephone. Planning with the writer is important and this should involve thinking about the follow-up activities.

Children should know something about the poet before the visit. The experience of having a poet in school will be much more worthwhile if the children have come across the work of the writer before the visit. There is greater anticipation and, being familiar with the poet's work, they can ask appropriate questions. I have been in a school where the teacher has informed the children, 'I have not read any of Mr Phinn's poetry but I am sure we will all enjoy the session.' Publishers very often are prepared to send publicity material—postcards, posters, flyers, bookmarks—which can be displayed alongside copies of the poet's work. The children and teachers might read and discuss some of the poems and prepare questions which they would like to ask. They might write some of their own poems based on the work of the visiting poet which they can read and show during the visit.

The visit

It is important that the poet is made to feel welcome when he or she walks through the door of the school. There might be a couple of pupils there to greet the visitor and introduce the headteacher and the teacher organising the day.

Arrangement for break times and lunch should be explained for the visiting poet might not be familiar with the routines of a particular school. He or she might also need to know certain things. For example, I was working in a school writing poems about grannies and grandpas and was not aware that a child in the group, who became distressed, had the day before attended her grandfather's funeral. Teachers might need to make the visiting poet aware of children who have special needs or some particular requirement.

A typical programme might include a talk to the whole school in assembly followed by workshops with smaller groups. The size of the workshop groups is an important factor to consider. Workshop activities are often intensive and require close and regular contact with each student. It is important to trust the poet. He or she will have worked in many schools, performing and running workshops, and will know what works and what programme will be appropriate and offer the best value for the children.

Ideally the poet should be given a spacious and attractive place in which to work. There should be a good supply of sharp pencils, erasers and paper, and wall space might be made available for a display. The school hall, which is often large and impersonal and might be needed to be cleared when lunch is being prepared, is far from ideal.

The teacher should be present at all times when the poet is performing or working with the children. There have been occasions when I have visited a school where the teacher has departed to catch up on his marking. Visiting writers are not supply teachers; being present means that the teacher can join in with the pupils and try his or her hand at writing too. Later he or she can work with the pupils on the follow-up work.

The local bookshop might provide some of the poet's books on a sale or return basis. Many children and teachers like to buy copies and have them signed during the visit. The poet might bring copies of his or her books for sale but children need to be reminded to bring some money if they wish to make a purchase.

After the visit

The follow-up of the visit is as important as the visit itself and can be wasted unless it is handled in a sensitive and imaginative way by the teacher involved. A visit where a poet inspires children and reads from his or her poems is all very well and is valuable in itself, but there could be an additional productive outcome where the teacher tries out some of the poet's suggestions, compiles a small anthology of the children's work and mounts a display. The children might write to the poet about the visit enclosing some of their efforts.

An evaluation of the visit is important. Has it challenged the students in new ways? Has it helped them to enjoy poetry more? Has it influenced their writing? There does not necessarily need to be a deal of writing from the children after the visit. If a pupil has written little in the workshop, he or she may have been stimulated in a way which will surface later in their work.

Chapter 24
Learning Poetry

Thoughts that breathe and words that burn.

Thomas Gray, 'The Progress of Poesy'

I can still recite some of the poems I learnt as a child, the nursery rhymes and riddles, tongue twisters and nonsense verse. At junior school, in an effort to rid us of our pronounced regional accent, the teacher would require us to chant various pieces of rhyming verse such as:

> Henry Hall hops on his heels.
> What an odd habit.
> How horrid it feels.
> Hopping on his heels
> Is not hopping at all,
> So why not hop properly, Henry Hall?

It was a fruitless exercise for us boys who delighted in converting it to our own Yorkshire version when were in the playground:

> 'Enery 'All 'ops on 'is 'eels.
> What an odd 'abit.
> 'Ow 'orrid hit feels.
> 'Oppin' on 'is 'eels
> Hisn't 'oppin' at all,
> So why not 'op properly, 'Enery 'All?

I disliked the elocution exercises and cannot say I was very keen either when we were compelled to learn by heart snatches of poetry. Now I am glad I did learn pieces of verse. As I travel down the motorway at dusk and see the moon high in the sky I find myself reciting bits of remembered verse: 'the moon like a ghostly galleon tossed upon cloudy seas'. As I stroll along a pebbly shore the words of a poem I learnt at school come to mind where 'the flung spray and the brown spume, and the seagulls crying'. Late at night when I put out the cat I recall the words of Walter de la Mare's beautiful poem: 'Slowly, silently, now the moon, walks the night in her silvery shoon'.

Children, I have found, do enjoy learning poems if it is not made too much of a chore. They love showing off their talents and performing the poems, particularly before their proud parents at school concerts.

One approach I have used to good effect is to give each child a large cut-out shape of a footprint. The children then scour the selection of poetry books made available and select a four-line (quatrain) poem they enjoy. In going through the books they come across lots of small poems—funny, sad, thoughtful, rhyming and non-rhyming. If the school does not have a rich selection of poetry books containing small verses, the teacher might make the selection herself and give each child a poem. The children write their chosen poems on the footprints in large bold letters and learn them. The footprints are then arranged across the classroom floor and a child is selected to remove his or her shoes and walk one by one along the footprints. When the traveller stops at a footprint the child who has written the poem on it recites the verse.

This is a fun activity and works with infants and juniors. I have used some traditional and perhaps less familiar short verses, anonymously written, which included:

TOMATO KETCHUP

If you do not shake the bottle,
None'll come, and then a lot'll.

PEAS

I eat my peas with honey,
I've done it all my life.
They do taste kind of funny,
But it keeps them on the knife.

GOD MADE THE BEES

God made the bees,
And the bees make honey.
The miller's man does all the work
But the miller makes the money.

A MAN IN THE WILD WOOD

A man in the wild wood asked of me,
'How many apples grow in the sea?'
I answered him as best as I could,
'As many fish that grow in the wood.'

WE WENT TO THE WOOD

We went to the wood and we caught it,
We all sat down and we sought it,
Because we could not find it
Home with us we brought it.

HUMPTY DUMPTY

Humpty Dumpty sat on a wall,
Eating black bananas.
Where do you think he puts the skins?
Down the king's pyjamas.

NO HARM DONE

As I went out the other day,
My head fell off and rolled away,
But when I noticed it was gone,
I picked it up and put it on.

AS I WAS GOING UP THE STAIR

As I was going up the stair
I met a man who wasn't there.
He wasn't there again today.
Oh, how I wish he'd go away.

ALGY

Algy met a grizzly bear
The grizzly bear met Algy.
The bear was bulgy
The bulge was Algy!

THERE WAS AN OLD WOMAN

There was an old woman
Who lived under the hill,
And if she's not gone,
She's living there still.

STAR LIGHT

Star light, star bright,
First star I see tonight,
I wish I may, I wish I might,
Have the wish I wish tonight.

HOW OLD ARE FLEAS?

Adam
Had 'em.

LESSON FROM THE SUNDIAL

Forget the rain, forget the showers,
Look forward to the sunshine hours.

DON'T CARE

Don't care was made to care,
Don't care was hung:
Don't care was put in a pot
And boiled till he was done.

A QUICK WAY OF COUNTING TO A HUNDRED

One, two,
Skip a few,
Ninety-nine, a hundred.

The following poems, written by myself, along with those by other poets, were performed at a parents' evening:

Infant Poems

I can do my buttons up,
I can tie my laces,
I can put my underpants on,
And I'm good at pulling faces.

Do not stare at the camel
As you are passing by,
For he will turn his dusty head
And spit you in the eye!

The elephant has no fingers,
The elephant has no toes,
But the elephant has enormous ears
And a very impressive nose.

(Published in *What I Like! Poems for the Very Young*
by Gervase Phinn, Child's Play International)

Junior Poems

SPELLING

The inspector asked the little ones
'Can anyone tell me,
A word that begins with the letter "Q"?'
And a child said, 'Quistmas Twee'.

(Published in *The Day Our Teacher Went Batty*
by Gervase Phinn, Puffin)

WHY?

Why do the white sails shiver?
What is that shaking on deck?
Why do the tall masts tremble?
Don't you know? It's a nervous wreck!

(Published in *Family Phantoms* by Gervase Phinn, Puffin)

There are many short poems ideal for this exercise in the following collections:

- *Short Poems: A Book of Very Short Poems* collected by Michael Harrison, Oxford University Press.

- *Silly Verse for Kids* by Spike Milligan, Puffin.

- *Mustard, Custard, Grumble Belly and Gravy* by Michael Rosen, illustrated by Quentin Blake, Bloomsbury Children's Books.

- *The Hat,* by Carol Ann Duffy, Faber & Faber.

- *Cat Among the Pigeons* by Kit Wright, illustrated by Posy Simmonds, Puffin.

- *100 Best Poems for Children*, edited by Roger McGough and illustrated by Sheila Moxley, Puffin.

- *Animal Lullabies*, *Wake Up, Sleepy Head* and *Animal Exercises: Poems to Keep Fit* by Mandy Ross, Child's Play International.

Chapter 25
Endpiece

Poetry needs to be at the heart of work in English because of the quality of the language at work. If language becomes separated from the moral and emotional life—becomes merely a string of clichés which neither communicate nor quicken the mind of the reader—then we run the risk of depriving children of the kind of vital resource of language which poetry can offer.

Teaching Poetry in the Secondary School: An HMI View,
Department for Education and Science (DES)

If as teachers we try to encourage children to turn to poetry as a source of enjoyment, we must ensure that this is matched by our own professional commitment. We must read poetry and know the range of anthologies available and what kind of poems interest and challenge our pupils. We must offer children a broad and balanced experience and they must see us enjoying poetry and hear us talk with some knowledge and enthusiasm about it and we must try our hand at writing poetry ourselves. If we do this then we will provide that vital resource of language which poetry can offer.

Twelve Edited Anthologies of Poetry

The books described below are those that many children have read and enjoyed and in some measure represent the great variety of verse now available. The list is very selective and contains only a small number of the many anthologies in print. It is not necessarily the best and I guess that some readers will feel some much-loved anthologies have been omitted. The list does, however, reflect ethnic diversity and contains contemporary publications as well as a range of traditional material. The question of the actual number of anthologies should be considered before anything else. Young children in particular will be overwhelmed by a large collection on the shelves and in the early years it is sensible to have a small but constantly-changing selection attractively displayed and accessible.

1   *100 Best Poems for Children*, edited by Roger McGough and illustrated by Sheila Moxley, Puffin

From the hundreds of poems originally chosen by children, Roger McGough has selected a rich and stimulating anthology of verse which includes the classic and the contemporary. Old favourites like 'The Highwayman', 'Matilda' and 'Albert and the Lion' are included along with poems by Terry Jones, Charles Causley, Jane and Ann Taylor and many more. There are poems of different lengths, moods and subjects, each one generously printed and beautifully illustrated.

2   *The Puffin Book of Fantastic First Poems*, edited by June Crebbin, Puffin

In her introduction June Crebbin writes: 'Here are poems which make me laugh out loud, or conjure up unforgettable images; poems that surprise me, or make me want to tap along with their rhythms; poems that stop me in my tracks, then linger in my mind.'

There is an enormous range of rich, original and varied poetry in this exciting and thought-provoking anthology. Featuring some of the best work of over sixty favourite children's poets, it includes funny, quirky, unusual, exciting, traditional and contemporary poems divided into seven sections. Children will come across animal poems, playtime poems, poems about family life and food, bedtime and outings, poems to sing, shout, whisper and chant and certainly enjoy.

June Crebbin was a primary school teacher and is now a full-time writer who visits schools to read, perform and talk about her poetry. Her publications include *The Jungle Sale*, *The Dinosaur's Dinner* and *Cows Moo, Cars Toot!*

3 *This Poem Doesn't Rhyme*, edited by Gerard Benson, Viking

Full of boisterous humour, this exciting and refreshing collection of non-rhyming poetry introduces children to the idea that poetry does not have to rhyme. There are examples of shape poems, dialogues, riddles, alliterative verse, lively rhythmic poems and gentle slow moving lyrics with a diversity of poets represented: John Wesley, Langston Hughes, Carl Sandburg, James Berry, E. E. Cummings, Edwin Morgan, Kathleen Raine, John Clare and some by the editor himself. 'What For', a poem by Noel Petty which appears in this collection, is one of the funniest and cleverest poems about parents that I have read.

4 *Poetry Jump Up: A Collection of Black Poetry*, compiled by Grace Nichols and illustrated by Michael Lewis, Penguin

This fresh, lively and diverse collection of poems by black writers from Britain, Africa, the US, Asia and the Caribbean, compiled by an award-winning poet, is full of life, colour and music. The poems range from the strongly rhythmic rhyming verse of Eloise Greenfield to the free verse poems of great poignancy and power of Maya Angelou. 'Just Because I Loves You' by Langston Hughes is a beautifully simple lyric, 'Don't Hit Your Sister' by Lesley Miranda and 'Feeding the Pastor' by Elma Stuckley are full of clever humour and 'My Country' written by Nelson Mandela's daughter Zinziswa, when she was twelve, is a small masterpiece.

In the foreword Grace Nichols writes: 'This [collection] is a way of offering children something new; new sounds and tastes and ways with words. I think it is important for all children to be exposed to poetry from different cultures.'

5 *Penguin's Poems for Life*, selected by Laura Barber, Penguin

'When we are young,' writes Laura Barber in the foreword to this anthology, 'we are quite used to the startling and stirring effect of poetry. It has a natural and instinctive place in our life: we taste the shape of words in our mouth, we feel the rhythms and we hear the rhymes. Discovering the right poem at the right time when you are older can be equally powerful and visceral.'

This splendidly rich and original anthology of contemporary and traditional poetry includes the whole gamut of verse—witty, sad, moving, magical, arresting, challenging, contemplative, clever and provocative—written by some of the finest and most popular poets. The poems vary in style and subject, some new but many familiar. If you are looking for a particular poem—'Jabberwocky' or 'If', 'To be, or not to be' or 'The Road Not Taken', 'The Owl and the Pussycat' or 'Don't Jump off the Roof Dad', it is likely to be in this collection.

6   *The Ring of Words: An Anthology of Poems for Children*, edited by Roger McGough, Faber & Faber

The big bright cover invites children to open this entertaining collection of appealing and original poems superbly illustrated with bold chalk drawings by Satoshi Kitamura. Robert Louis Stevenson, Walter de la Mare, James Berry, Jackie Kay, Joyce Grenfell, Vernon Scannell, R. S. Thomas, Brian Patten and many other fine poets celebrate shoes and soldiers, bears and bullies, mice and mothers, cats and cold feet.

7   *Magic Poems*, *Family Poems*, *Animal Poems* and *School Poems*, compiled by Jennifer Curry, Scholastic

This fresh and wide-ranging series of edited poetry books are guaranteed to make children think and respond. There are palindromes, shape poems, snapshots, rhyming and non-rhyming verse, some written by well-known poets and some by children.

8   *The Oxford Book of Children's Poetry*, edited by Michael Harrison and Christopher Stuart-Clark, Oxford University Press

The editors offer a range of carefully and imaginatively selected poems in this challenging and refreshing anthology, which includes the classic favourites and fresh new discoveries. The contributors, which include Jenny Joseph and Jackie Kay, Adrian Henri and Ian McMillan, Brian Patten and Elizabeth Jennings, come from around the world and write with power and passion, with great sensitivity and humour. This anthology is as rich and varied in language as it is diverse in themes and includes limericks, narrative poems, nonsense verse, ballads and songs.

9   *Crack Another Yolk and Other Word Play Poems*, compiled by John Foster, Oxford University Press

This collection is a treasure house of dynamic and diverse poems sure to interest and excite young readers. Rhymes, jingles, jokes, tricks, puns, acrostics, riddles, limericks, calligrams, epitaphs, counting rhymes, word puzzles, miniature poems, haiku and many more verse forms show children just how varied poetry can be.

10   *Thoughts Like an Ocean,* poems chosen by Neil Nuttall and Andy Hawkins, and illustrated by Jenny Fell, Pont

Many anthologies for children feature the well-known and much enjoyed poets like Michael Rosen, Roger McGough, Jackie Kay and June Crebbin. This fresh and lively compilation contains the verse of largely unfamiliar poets and it is a delight. There are cosy and amusing poems, poems which disturb and challenge and some beautifully quiet and descriptive verse. Babies and bullies, saints and snowmen, witches and football heroes, conkers and rainbows and many more themes are explored. There are so many sure-fire winners in this collection but try the brilliant 'The Goat of Many Colours' by Alun Perry and the poignant 'Harry Pushed Her' by Peter Thabit Jones.

11   *Short Poems: A Book of Very Short Poems*, collected by Michael Harrison, Oxford University Press

> All the poems in this book are very short.
> Some are only three words long.
> But they say a lot.
> Try one!

Every classroom should have a copy of this collection. There are eighty short poems on all sorts of subjects from caterpillars to cats, mermaids to dragons, frogs to owls, radishes to dandelions. There are clever, amusing, witty poems as well as the serious, poignant and thoughtful by a whole host of poets: Hilaire Belloc, U. A. Fanthorpe, Judith Nicholls, Adrian Mitchell, Gerard Manley Hopkins, Ian Serraillier, Christina Rossetti, Robert Graves, Brian Patten, Ogden Nash, D. H. Lawrence, Carl Sandburg, Edward Thomas, Robert Frost, Robert Louis Stevenson and many more.

12   *I've Got a Poem for You: Poems to Perform*, collected by John Foster and illustrated by Belle Mellor, Oxford University Press

Over forty new and traditional poems have been collected together with skill and imagination by the poet and compiler John Foster. The wide range of verse forms represented conveys the vibrancy and richness of the English language, showing how metre, rhyme and rhythm combine to create clever and memorable verse. Raps, prayers, conversation poems, ballads, legends, songs and carols are ideal for performing. There is a good balance between the serious and comic, the formal and informal, the immediate and contemplative.

Twelve Individual Poetry Collections

1   *Mustard, Custard, Grumble Belly and Gravy* by Michael Rosen, illustrated by Quentin Blake, Bloomsbury Children's Books

In his introduction to this bright, accessible anthology (a combination of his two previous collections, *You Can't Catch Me* and *Don't Put Mustard in the Custard*) Michael Rosen writes: 'What I've written here will give you the material for a whole number of bedtime, car-journey or classroom performances. Like most poets I have a go at writing about a variety of things in a variety of ways.'

And there is real variety here. With spontaneous freshness Michael Rosen conjures up the brightest and clearest of pictures of family life, school and the wide world around us. He has a real insight into and understanding of the feelings and thoughts of children and catches their imaginations in this observant and original collection. There is a wealth of poems about shoes and shorts, noses and nightmares, babies and bullies and the collection is peopled by a wonderful cast of characters—Johnny and JoJo and Jim and Danny. 'I'm Big' and 'Keith's Cupboard' are two of my all-time favourites.

2   *Ted Hughes: Collected Poems for Children*, illustrated by Raymond Briggs, Faber & Faber

The poems of Ted Hughes engage, challenge and delight children and this superb collection contains a vast range of his humorous and inventive verse about the natural world. Illustrated by the incomparable Raymond Briggs, who has produced some of the most celebrated and cherished picture books so loved by children (and adults), this anthology brings together the children's poetry Ted Hughes wrote throughout his life. Beginning with those for younger readers such as 'Hermit Crab' and 'Conger Eel', they progress to the more complex and thoughtful poems of 'A Cranefly in September' and 'The Seven Sorrows'. I once attended a school concert called 'I Must Go Down to the Sea Again' where children, dressed as various sea creatures, gave readings and recited poems about the ocean, some of which were by Ted Hughes. I particularly liked the small boy performing 'Jellyfish' who stated somewhat lugubriously:

> Though I look like a slob,
> It's a delicate job
> Being just a blob.

3   *Collected Poems of Allan Ahlberg*, Puffin

No classroom or library poetry collection would be complete without a selection of Alan Ahlberg's verse which has delighted generations of children and adults alike over a period of twenty-five years. Described as 'clever, funny and nostalgic' (*Sunday Times*) and 'hilarious and poignant' (*Guardian*), his poems have done more than any others to make poetry accessible for young readers. His rhythms, rhymes, images and ideas are irresistible. Children delight in his humour, love the catchy rhymes and identify with the moods and feelings he so skilfully captures. This collection, superbly illustrated by Charlotte Voake, winner of the WH Smith Illustration Award, is a beautifully bound collection of his five books of verse, including the classic *Please Mrs Butler*, voted the most important twentieth century children's poetry book in the Books for Keeps poll.

I have used many of Allan Ahlberg's verses as stimuli for children's own verse writing. As a starting point, try giving children the titles of some of the poems and asking them to try to compose a short piece of verse: 'I Did a Bad Thing Once'; 'Dog in the Playground'; 'Back to School'; 'Things I Have Been Doing Lately'. This can be tried with opening lines as well: 'Upon that dark and frosty eve ...', 'The teacher said ...', 'She came into the classroom ...', 'Sometimes when I'm in trouble ...'.

Another of Allan Ahlberg's collections is a sure-fire winner with boys: *Friendly Matches* is a clever, funny and nostalgic celebration in verse of football.

4   *Wicked World!* by Benjamin Zephaniah, Puffin

> All people are people
> And as far as I can see
> You're all related to me
> That is why I say that
> All people are equal.

This delightfully inventive collection full of sparkling language, vibrant rhythms and shrewd insight demands to be read and rapped. There are poems such as 'I Luv Me

Mudder' and 'Bengali Rap' which are ideal for performance and others such as 'We Refugees' and 'Children of the Sewers' which are poignant and thoughtful and will generate lively discussion. Every classroom should have a copy of this warm, compassionate and imaginative collection by one of the country's greatest poets.

5   *Red, Cherry Red* by Jackie Kay, illustrated by Rob Ryan,
     Bloomsbury Publishing Plc

'I always looked out at the world and wondered if the world looked back at me,' writes this award-winning Scottish poet. Brilliant, challenging and wonderfully evocative these poems tell us of Jackie Kay's world, a world of fearsome Mrs Dungeon Brae who lived on the Isle of Mull; the woman who guts the herring, 'pulling the innards oot, day in day oot'; the fisherman who recalls 'the cut of the cliff, steaming with spray'; the bird-like Aunt Peggy 'who flaps about when the phone rings'; and Great Grandmother with the 'bony hands' and the 'round shoulders and sticky oot back'.

I have had great fun getting children to have a go at reading, with a Scottish accent of course, the uproarious 'Hauf a Dozen' which begins:

> My maw telt me tae buy:
> hauf a dozen eggs,
> a big bag o' tatties,
> a loaf o' bread, an a tin o' beans,
> and tae check ma change
> an I wuid get sixpence.

6   *Cat Among the Pigeons* by Kit Wright, illustrated by Posy Simmonds, Puffin

Kit Wright's verse has all the qualities which appeal to children: simplicity, a sense of drama, strong regular rhythms, echoing rhymes and originality of expression. Here are poems which cover a wide range of themes and emotions—poems about things we like and things we hate, familiar sayings and daily events, eccentric people and strange animals. There is the nasty old woman who lived in Accrington and the incorrigible Dave Dirt, mad dinner ladies and the infuriating little brother who is forever picking his nose. There are singing spuds and miserable prawns, singing hedgehogs and tough limpets.

Kit Wright is well known for his popular collections such as *Hot Dog and Other Poems* and his anthologies such as *The New Puffin Book of Funny Verse* as well as being in big demand as a performer and teacher.

7   *Silly Verse for Kids* by Spike Milligan, Puffin

In the foreword Spike Milligan writes: 'Most of these poems were written to amuse my children; some were written as a result of things they said in the home. No matter what you say, my kids think I'm brilliant!'

All children think Spike Milligan's verse is brilliant. His ridiculous rhymes, illustrated with his own absurd drawings, never fail to amuse and delight. Brimming with laughter and fun, these clever, bizarre, wildly inventive poems have a long-lasting appeal for children and are particularly popular with those who are poetry resistant.

8   *The Tale of Tales* by Tony Mitton, illustrated by Peter Bailey, Corgi

This is a beautifully illustrated, affectionate and witty collection by one of the finest children's writers. Young readers are quick to appreciate the humour and magic of the verse and come to love the rhymes and rhythms. They will also be captivated by the compelling story of Monkey, Elephant and their friends as they journey to Volcano Valley in search of the greatest story of them all—the Tale of Tales.

9   *The Tortoise had a Mighty Roar* by Peter Dixon, illustrated by David Thomas, Macmillan

Children love the humour, cleverness of language, the rhymes and rhythms of Peter Dixon's vibrant verse. Wild, wonderful and exaggerated characters abound on page after page. There's Big Billy, the spider with legs as thick as a rope, and clever William who wrote things with a quill but couldn't do the SATs. There's the Human Knot who gets in a terrible tangle and Houdini who finds himself locked in Grandma's loo. Peter Dixon's verse collection is excellent for introducing children to the whole range of poetry: sad and serious poems like 'Collecting Time' and 'Wildlife' sit alongside manic and hilarious verses like 'World Book Day Party' and 'Excuses'. Offbeat, amusing and original, this collection is enhanced superbly by the quirky and endearing illustrations of David Thomas.

A former lecturer in education, Peter Dixon travels the world visiting schools and colleges to perform his poetry and he is one of the most popular and entertaining speakers at education conferences.

10   *The Hat* by Carol Ann Duffy, Faber & Faber

Lively, clever, witty, moving and endearing, this collection is essential reading, taking children on a joyous journey through sand and schoolrooms, socks and songs where they discover an enchanting and imaginative world. At the heart of the book is the hat which is blown through history landing on one literary head after another and quoting the wearer's famous lines as it comes to rest. These original and inventive poems for children are full of engaging humour and lively language.

11   *Animal Lullabies, Wake Up, Sleepy Head* and *Animal Exercises: Poems to Keep Fit* by Mandy Ross, Child's Play International

Mandy Ross's three bright, beautifully illustrated collections are massively appealing to young children. There is a sharp, matter-of-fact freshness in her delightfully warm, witty and appealing poems. Every teacher of the early years should have these splendidly rich resources in her or his desk drawer or on the bookshelf to read at odd moments and encourage the children to delight in the clever language and unusual imagery. The collections also offer perfect bedtime opportunities for parents.

12   *Stars, Cars, Electric Guitars* by James Carter, Walker Books

> I was rummaging around
> inside my head
> looking for something
> I'd forgotten
>
> and there were so many
> things up there—

So writes the poet. In this original, funny and very accessible collection of largely shape poems, we join James Carter on his search and find crisps and garden sheds, shooting stars and clouds, windows and vacuum cleaners, teardrops and baubles. We meet Darren the Dolphin, the girl with the blue glasses, Noah and Alan Greenwood. Children love the sound, speed, action and humour of James Carter's poetry, published in this collection in bold and diverse print.

About the Author

In addition to contributing to over a hundred poetry anthologies, Gervase Phinn has edited five collections of poems and published five of his own. He runs workshops in schools, speaks at conferences and has directed courses on the teaching of poetry for many years. **www.gervase-phinn.com**

Acknowledgements

The author wishes to thank:

- The many children who have granted permission for their poetry to be used in this book.

- The many talented teachers he has met for their time and cooperation.

- Christine Jopling and Chris Mould for permission to use their glorious illustrations.

- All of the publishers and galleries who have given permission for material to be used in this book.

- The editor of this collection for her encouragement, good humour, advice and patience.

Thank you all.

Praise for *Teaching Poetry in the Primary Classroom*

"Poetry has had a hard time in schools in recent years, subjected to analysis, synthesis, interpretation and dissection and all in the services of literacy. With this book Gervase exuberantly, vividly and with great practicality reveals his philosophy of work and pleasure going hand in hand. He emphasises enthusiasm with joy, delight, wonder and fun permeating everything in developing both skills and knowledge. This book is a life-line: grasp it!"

Chris Brown, Review Editor of *The School Librarian*
and former Primary Headteacher

"Gervase Phinn has drawn on his experience as a teacher, adviser, school inspector and poet to produce this useful book which provides teachers with an invaluable way of approaching poetry in the primary classroom. He shows teachers how to encourage children to enjoy reading and writing poetry. Phinn believes that poetry should be experienced before it is analysed and that 'close study at an early age' is not the way to encourage enjoyment.

The bulk of the book is made up of chapters covering different kinds of poems and the limericks, clerihews, ballads, acrostic poems, alphabet poems and so on are accompanied by a mass of poems, many of them his own work. The poet is keen to follow through on the way he himself was taught which made 'the pleasure principle paramount'. The book is intended to enable teachers to provide a rich diet of poetry for children. At a time of mounting concern about the way poetry is approached, this helpful book provides an essential handbook for primary schools. No classroom should be without it."

Chris Holifield, Director of the Poetry Book Society,
which runs the Children's Poetry Bookshelf

"I have sploshed many a damp mile with the author of this book, seeking precious jet on Yorkshire shores. Also ancient ammonites on bracing beaches and shin-crack rocks. Together we have sipped amber ales in evening hostelries and competed fiercely for the wildest and funniest tales of infant class or irate governor including Darren's trousers, headless donkeys or, of course, the Ofsted lady and the papier mache accident. Personally, I recall with pride being the regular winner of the largest lump of jet or finest ammonite award and, just occasionally, having the funniest school assembly or dinner lady story award.

I must, however, admit to being an all time runner up when it comes to the 'teaching of poetry in the classroom' event. For teaching poetry with class 3 Mr Phinn gets the gold medal, podium man. Well done Gervase! I found Teaching Poetry in the Primary School hugely readable and just the sort of book that every teacher should take with them on their next trip to the Yorkshire Dales or N.U.T. coach tour. Tons of ideas, plus plentiful laughs and gentle tears.

And MOST IMPORTANTLY OF ALL, guess what? I have not found an ounce, gram or fairy thimbleful of National Curriculum wordage creeping into the text. There are no cringingly awful and off-putting page headings blazoning AIMS AND TARGETS, OBJECTIVES OR ASSESSMENTS, no nasty literacy hour headings or infringements to besmirch the pure pleasure of poetry reading and writing, nothing to weary the spirit of simply enjoying a poem, and learning how to write a poem for the joy of doing so. So follow the rhyme, enjoy the read. Buy the book and get a pen. Have a go! And take the children with you. This book is for every child in every home or school, dog in kennel or ant in hill. It is for you. It is for word, jet and fossil hunters. Everywhere."

Peter Dixon, Poet, Education Consultant

Further Reading

Selected poems in this book were taken from the following poetry books by Gervase Phinn.

A Wayne in a Manger

ISBN: 978-014102688-6

It Takes One to Know One

ISBN: 978-014130901-9

Don't Tell the Teacher

ISBN: 978-014132074-8

Family Phantoms

ISBN: 978-014131446-4

The Day Our teacher Went Batty

ISBN: 978-014131445-7

What I like: Poems for the Very Young

ISBN: 978-190455012-9